JANICE THOMPSON

unstoppable
GOD

Hope-Filled
Devotions & Prayers
for Women

BARBOUR
PUBLISHING

Print ISBN 978-1-63609-282-9

Published by Barbour Publishing, Inc., 1810 Barbour Drive, Uhrichsville, Ohio 44683, www.barbourbooks.com

Our mission is to inspire the world with the life-changing message of the Bible.

Printed in China.

INTRODUCTION

God is unstoppable!

Stop and think about that for a moment. What you lack in perseverance, He more than makes up for! He never quits. Your heavenly Father is on the job 24–7, 365 days a year. Best of all, He never gives up on you, even when you give up on yourself. He's a persistent, never-say-never Father, and He's ready to pour out that same persistence on you, His daughter.

If you want to live an unstoppable life, then becoming more like God is key. In this easy-to-use devotional, you'll find example after example, story after story, of your unstoppable heavenly Father! When you feel like giving up—on life, on relationships, on your workload—turn to the truths found in His Word. They will bring comfort and hope and assure you that you are not alone. (Hey, we all feel hopeless from time to time!)

God is unstoppable. And because you're created in His image, you can be unstoppable too!

"I know that you can do everything and
that your plans are unstoppable."
JOB 42:2 GW

GOD IS STILL WORKING ON YOU

We are his workmanship, created in Christ Jesus for good works,
which God prepared beforehand, that we should walk in them.

EPHESIANS 2:10 ESV

Have you ever started a project but not finished it? Maybe you wanted to renovate a room in your home. Or clean out your garage. Or delve into the world of scrapbooking. But you lost interest quickly and left a mess in your wake.

We're not always great at completing tasks, but God excels at it! He has started many wonderful things in you, and your unstoppable God isn't ready to give up on you yet (even though you've been ready to give up on yourself a time or two). Nope. He's hanging in there, still working on you, honing and perfecting those areas you've struggled in.

Does it give you courage and hope to know that your Master Creator is still hard at work on you? It should! He's not giving up, and neither should you.

I'm an unfinished work, but I'm counting on You
to finish what You've started, Lord! Amen.

THERE'S NO PLACE GOD WON'T GO TO FIND YOU

Where can I go from your Spirit? Where can I flee from
your presence? If I go up to the heavens, you are there;
if I make my bed in the depths, you are there.

PSALM 139:7–8 NIV

There's no hide-and-seek with God. He always finds you, even when you burrow down deep, thinking you can't be found. His all-seeing eye is right there, watching over you, whispering, *"Give it up, kid! I'm onto you! And you can never hide from Me."*

Don't be spooked by this revelation! He's hunting you down, not to scold but to show you just how loved you are! Your unstoppable God isn't resting even when you're at the giving-up point. His love penetrates the darkness and keeps going. . .and going. . .and going.

Think of the many times you've tried to hide from Him. Did it work? (Nope!) Instead of running away from the Lord, maybe it's time to run straight into His arms. There you will find the healing you need. (And face it, you'll be saving God a lot of time and trouble by not running!)

Lord, I'm sorry for the times I tried to run and hide. Thank
You for chasing me down. Your love is unstoppable! Amen.

GOD STOPS AT NOTHING

"For God so loved the world, that he gave his only Son, that whoever believes in him should not perish but have eternal life."

JOHN 3:16 ESV

If you're a lover of people, John 3:16 probably remains on your "favorites" list. When you truly love people as God does, then you do whatever it takes to reach them. You stop at nothing.

That's the kind of love your heavenly Father showed you when He gave His only Son, Jesus. He looked at you and said, *"I'm not letting this one go. I won't quit even if she does. I'll give the one thing that means the most to Me—My child—so that she can share eternity with Me."*

Wow! Doesn't that thrill your soul? No matter the hour, no matter the situation, He's simply not giving up on you. And that free gift of salvation—purchased through the death of His Son on the cross—sealed the deal.

Now it's your turn! If God won't give up on you, perhaps it's time to acknowledge that you shouldn't give up on yourself either. Or on Him. Or on others. Today, ask your unstoppable God to make you more like Him so that you have that never-give-up attitude.

Lord, thank You for the gift of salvation! I'm so grateful for the work of the Savior on the cross. To think He did it all for me! Amen.

GOD PURCHASED YOU BACK

When the LORD began to speak through Hosea, the LORD said to him, "Go, marry a promiscuous woman and have children with her, for like an adulterous wife this land is guilty of unfaithfulness to the LORD." So he married Gomer daughter of Diblaim, and she conceived and bore him a son.

HOSEA 1:2–3 NIV

Hosea, a man of God, received a very unusual message: *"Go marry a prostitute."* Can you imagine the inner turmoil he must have faced? "Um, God. . .are You sure?"

Instead of arguing, he took Gomer as his wife. They settled down and had a family, and then the unthinkable happened. She decided to go back to her old life. Gomer disappeared from her husband and children and plummeted straight back into the things that once bound her.

Maybe you've been there. You've returned to a former habit. An old sin. An addictive lifestyle you thought you'd escaped.

Hosea found his bride—haggard and broken—on the auction block. Instead of turning his back on her, ashamed by her choices, he purchased her back. Compelled by love, he stopped at nothing to claim the heart of his bride.

What a lovely picture of God's love for us, His children. Like Hosea, the Lord purchased you back, girl! What a forgiving, loving Father!

I've tumbled pretty far, Lord. I've gone to the depths of sin and despair. But You found me there and bought me back. Thank You, my unstoppable God! Amen.

CHASING DOWN THE ONE

Then Jesus told them this parable: "Suppose one of you has a hundred sheep and loses one of them. Doesn't he leave the ninety-nine in the open country and go after the lost sheep until he finds it? And when he finds it, he joyfully puts it on his shoulders and goes home. Then he calls his friends and neighbors together and says, 'Rejoice with me; I have found my lost sheep.' "

LUKE 15:3–6 NIV

Jesus is in the business of tracking down His missing sheep. Maybe you've been that little lamb at times! Your unstoppable Shepherd has His staff in hand and is calling your name. He has ventured to the edge of the field to find you, so come out from behind that bush! Stop hiding in the hedges! He's on to you, girl!

Why does the Shepherd care enough to leave the ninety-nine to find the one? We'll never know, though we have a strong hint in Genesis where we learn that we were created in His image. We do know that His love for the one (you!) is magnificent. It defies explanation. It goes to the heights, the depths, and the broadest widths to make sure you're taken care of.

Surely, if the Creator cares for His created, then we can learn to care too! May we be unstoppable in wooing back the lost, those who have ventured far from the flock.

Jesus, be my guide! Show me how to pursue the lost sheep the way You do! Amen.

EVEN THEN. . .HE LOVED

The true light that gives light to everyone was coming into the world. He was in the world, and though the world was made through him, the world did not recognize him.

JOHN 1:9–10 NIV

Even before creation, God cared. Before a single blade of grass covered a patch of ground, before an iridescent fish swam in a tumultuous sea, the Creator loved. That love has transcended time as we know it—billowing past Adam and Eve's original sin and traveling through the generations of mankind.

God hasn't given up on us, folks. He didn't give up on Jonah. Or David. Or Samson. He didn't give up on Peter. Or even Judas. His transcendent love stretched across all those eras, all those people, and reaches to you, today.

Before creation, God knew you and loved you. He stood ready to chase you down should the need arise. That's the kind of unstoppable God you serve. With effortless grace, He descends into your situation and whispers, *"Hey, you. . .yes, you! I'm right here, and I'm not going anywhere."* What joy to love a God like that!

Lord, thank You for traveling across time to pour out Your love on me! How grateful I am. Amen.

DOES GOD REACH
A BREAKING POINT?

*The LORD regretted that he had made human beings on the
earth, and his heart was deeply troubled. So the LORD said,
"I will wipe from the face of the earth the human race I have
created—and with them the animals, the birds and the creatures
that move along the ground—for I regret that I have made
them." But Noah found favor in the eyes of the LORD.*

GENESIS 6:6–8 NIV

Have you ever wondered why God hasn't zapped us all? We're a hot
mess, for sure, and rarely live according to the map He's laid out for
us. We tend to go our own way and do our own thing—to His sadness
and our detriment.

Back in Noah's time, God really did reach a breaking point. He'd
had it with the sin of mankind and actually regretted creating man in
the first place. He decided to wipe out creation. But then something
rather remarkable happened. A lone man named Noah found favor
in the eyes of the Lord.

Our unstoppable God looked down onto the heart of this one
man and said, *"This one gives me hope that life really should go on."* And
because of the actions of one man, we all exist today.

Wow! Our unstoppable God could have wiped out all traces of
humanity, but His deep love for Noah kept our story going. How
precious is His great love for us even when we mess up!

*Lord, I know I've strayed so many times. Thank You
for not giving up on me! Thanks for giving me chance
after chance. How grateful I am! Amen.*

YOU CAN RUN, BUT. . .

The word of the LORD came to Jonah son of Amittai: "Go to the great city of Nineveh and preach against it, because its wickedness has come up before me." But Jonah ran away from the LORD and headed for Tarshish. He went down to Joppa, where he found a ship bound for that port. After paying the fare, he went aboard and sailed for Tarshish to flee from the LORD.

JONAH 1:1–3 NIV

Have you ever heard the expression "You can run, but you can't hide"? It's true, especially when God is the one doing the chasing.

Sometimes the Lord gives us our marching orders and we don't like them. Such was the case with Jonah. He heard God's plan—to offer a second chance to the people of Nineveh—and said, "Nope. Not gonna help You out with this one, Lord."

So he ran. To Joppa. Then on board a ship to Tarshish. From there he was propelled overboard and ended up in the belly of a big fish.

The people of Nineveh weren't the only ones to whom God offered a second chance. He gave Jonah an opportunity to make things right. In the end, the big fish spit him up (ew!) and he got back on the road to Nineveh, a contrite heart leading the way. That's how it is with our unstoppable God! We run. He catches us. We have a "come to Jesus" meeting.

Been there, done that, Lord! I'll do my best not to make You chase me down from now on! Amen.

UNSTOPPABLE LOVE

*"Greater love has no one than this,
that someone lay down his life for his friends."*

JOHN 15:13 ESV

Our unstoppable God offers us unstoppable love. Think about it: He continues to pour it out—like water rushing over a waterfall—even when we don't deserve it.

Why does God's vast love for His creation continue to flow? Why doesn't He dam up the river and withhold love from us the way we tend to do with those who disappoint us? Because God is incapable of turning His back—or His heart—on His creation. He simply cannot do that. His adoration is a part of His character. And because we're created in His image, it needs to be part of our character too.

Can you love with the same unstoppable love God has shown you? This might seem an impossible task, but God longs for you to try. When people hurt you. When you're disappointed by their actions. Even when your heart is broken. Keep loving, girl. Keep pouring it out even when it hurts.

Unstoppable love. It's how God longs for us to live.

Show me how, Jesus! I want to love like You do! Amen.

LOVE NEVER FAILS

Love is patient and kind; love does not envy or boast; it is not arrogant or rude. It does not insist on its own way; it is not irritable or resentful; it does not rejoice at wrongdoing, but rejoices with the truth. Love bears all things, believes all things, hopes all things, endures all things. Love never ends. As for prophecies, they will pass away; as for tongues, they will cease; as for knowledge, it will pass away.

1 CORINTHIANS 13:4–8 ESV

Love never fails. No doubt you've read that verse or heard it quoted as part of a wedding ceremony or vow renewal. When you truly love—the sacrificial way God intended—anything is possible. Broken friendships can be restored. Marriages can be put back together. Parents and children can cohabitate without constant bickering. Love is the superglue that holds all things together in good times and bad.

If love never fails, then imagine what unstoppable love would do! If we *really* loved as much, as often, as deeply as God does, then squabbles would be a thing of the past. Selfishness would disappear off the planet. The "me first" mentality would cease. Wow! What a different world we would live in!

Oh, to love as He loves! Oh, to spread that kind of love everywhere we go—like bread crumbs of hope for this lost, aching world!

Jesus, I want to love unconditionally but need Your help! Your love never fails. Teach me how to be unstoppable in my love for You and for others. Amen.

LOVE, THE PERFECT BINDER

And above all these put on love, which binds
everything together in perfect harmony.
COLOSSIANS 3:14 ESV

Quilters know a secret that the rest of us don't—a lovely quilt holds together much better when you add a binder. To create the binder, a separate piece of fabric, long and narrow, is sewn to the outside edges of the quilt on all sides. In essence, it holds things together. Without it, those fabric blocks would lose their shape. They would end up catawampus!

Chefs often "bind" their creations as well. When baking cookies or cakes, they often use eggs to hold the other ingredients together. Skip the binder and your sweets won't bake up the same.

What is the great "binder" that Jesus recommends? Love, of course! When all else fails, love succeeds. It's the fabric holding the quilt of life together. It's the missing ingredient when you're baking up a new relationship. When you "put on" love, everything holds together in perfect harmony. Our unstoppable God knows the ultimate secret—unstoppable love really does hold all things together!

I get it, Lord! When I love like You do, all areas of my life come together
seamlessly! Thank You for showing me how to love this way. Amen.

KEEP ON

"I give you a new Law. You are to love each other. You must love each other as I have loved you. If you love each other, all men will know you are My followers."

JOHN 13:34–35 NLV

Unstoppable love seems impossible at times. When you're cranky. When you're exhausted. When you've given multiple chances and the person keeps letting you down. It's easier to turn and walk away.

That's not God's way, though. He keeps going. . .and going. . .and going. He's like the Energizer Bunny, never willing to give up! And He's hoping you'll follow His lead. Why? Because this is how the world will know that He exists. When you love others the way He does, people sit up and take notice. They say things like, "Hey, did you see how kindly she treated that mean coworker?" or "Whoa. I don't think I'd have that kind of patience!"

The world is watching. They can catch glimpses of our unstoppable God if we live the way He has called us to live. Keep loving. Keep forgiving. Keep hoping for the best. By doing so, you'll be sharing hope with a lost world.

I get it, Jesus. All eyes are on me, and that's okay as long as I'm pointing them to You! Amen.

A BLANKET OF LOVE

Above all, keep loving one another earnestly,
since love covers a multitude of sins.

1 PETER 4:8 ESV

Love is the whipped cream on top of your proverbial pie of life. (Yum!) It's a lovely covering, the perfect creamy topping to go over all that icky stuff life throws your way. Love truly does cover sins. And pain. And broken relationships. And disappointments. And fear. It's the sweetness on top of the icky, the joy on top of the mourning. And it's yours for the taking.

Love is like a warm, fuzzy blanket that covers you when you need it most. There are no holes. No broken threads. No tattered hems. Unquenchable love—poured out from your unstoppable God—is never going to quit working, no matter what life throws at it. It's the perfect covering for whatever you might be going through, even now, at this very moment.

Love covers everything.

Jesus, thank You for the reminder that Your unstoppable love
is enough! It covers my troubles, my broken heart, even my
deepest hidden pain. I can trust Your love, Lord! Amen.

HARMONY

*Live in harmony with one another. Do not be haughty, but associate
with the lowly. Never be wise in your own sight. Repay no one evil
for evil, but give thought to do what is honorable in the sight of all.
If possible, so far as it depends on you, live peaceably with all.*

ROMANS 12:16–18 ESV

If you've ever arrived at the theater a few minutes before the play
begins, you've probably heard the orchestra warming up. Talk about
an odd cacophony of sounds! It's anything but pleasing to the ears as
the instrument voices overlap one another.

The same is true of unharmonious relationships. With so many
voices vying for attention, it's hard to know who to listen to. Or what
to believe. Or how to fix it.

Aren't you glad your unstoppable God is relentless when it comes
to fixing broken relationships? He wants us to be relentless too! His
ultimate desire is for His kids to wear love like a cloak so that it is
visible to all. This kind of love is only possible through Him. So do
what is honorable in the sight of all. Wrap yourself in unstoppable love.

*Father, I thank You for Your relentless pursuit of harmony! May I
pursue it too, with Your unstoppable love leading the way. Amen.*

THIS IS HOW THEY WILL KNOW

"A new commandment I give to you, that you love one another: just as I have loved you, you also are to love one another. By this all people will know that you are my disciples, if you have love for one another."

JOHN 13:34–35 ESV

By *this* all people will know that we are His disciples—when we love.

The world is watching. They're looking for living, breathing demonstrations of God's unstoppable love. Many don't hold out hope that they will witness it firsthand, but as a child of the King, you have the opportunity to prove them wrong! By loving (even when it makes no sense), you show the world that you're like Jesus.

Have love for one another. Even when you don't always agree. Even when you're having a rough day. Even when differences in philosophy exist. Love one another. When times are good and when times are rough.

This is how they will know.

Lord, I want to set an example for the world, to show them Your unstoppable love! You've commanded me to love. No questions asked. Help me live it out, I pray. Today, rid me of pride. Get rid of my haughty spirit. May nothing but love remain. Amen.

THE GREATEST IS LOVE

And now we have these three: faith and hope
and love, but the greatest of these is love.

1 CORINTHIANS 13:13 NLV

There are some really great things you could celebrate: friendship, romance, your paycheck, opportunities, joys, second chances.

Yes, life gives you plenty of reasons to offer up a shout of praise. Things are great! But no matter how many "good things" you experience, there's one that tops them all—love.

Love is greater than great. It rises to the top like fresh cream. It's better than faith, better than hope, better than all the joys of life rolled into one. Love never fails, which is why it tops the list. You can't lose when you incorporate godly love into the situations you face.

How does that play out in your life? How can you exhibit love? Today would be a great day to ask the Lord to show you. He'll give you thousands of opportunities to respond out of great love for others and for Him.

Your love is the greatest thing I have to offer this world, Jesus!
Thank You for reminding me that it tops the list! Amen.

LOVE COVERS OFFENSES

Hatred stirs up strife, but love covers all offenses.
PROVERBS 10:12 ESV

God is unstoppable in so many different ways. He pursues you even when you don't want Him to! His love is truly the most powerful force in your life, greater than any weapon you could ever use.

One of the key ways God's love operates is through forgiveness. You know how it is. A little disagreement between friends turns into an offense. Before long, space grows up between you. The chasm deepens. After a while, you barely speak.

God's love is powerful enough to penetrate through the offense and calm troubled waters. It can smooth out the rough places and make things right between you again. That unstoppable love can cover the offense and mend broken hearts. Yes, it's really that powerful.

Who do you need to forgive today? Is there someone whose words cut you to the quick? It's time to let it go, sweet woman of God. And while you're at it, ask the Lord to show you who you might have offended. Perhaps there are people out there who struggle with some things you've said as well.

Love never fails. It covers offenses. And pain. And heartache. Give His unstoppable love a try today.

*Lord, today I choose to let go of the offenses I've held
on to for so long. May Your overflowing, unstoppable
love do its deepest work in my heart, I pray. Amen.*

25

HE CAN SHOW YOU HOW

Dear friends, let us continue to love one another, for love comes from God. Anyone who loves is a child of God and knows God.

1 JOHN 4:7 NLT

Some folks just aren't easy to love. They're socially awkward. They say the wrong things, offend people, stir up grief and trouble. And yet God calls you to love them with the same unstoppable love you pour out on those who are easy.

"How, Lord?" you ask. It seems impossible!

Here's the good news: God can show you how—in each situation and with every unbearable case. He can show you the best possible way to express love, even to the ones who seem impossible. Love is "of" God. It comes from Him. If He's capable of loving the unlovable, then you must be too!

Whoever loves has been born of God and knows God. Think about that for a moment. When you take the time to love the difficult ones, you're becoming more like your Creator. You're showing Him—and the world—that you're truly His child, operating out of the same love He's always expressed to you (even when you didn't deserve it).

Beloved, let us love one another.

It is possible with His unstoppable love.

Lord, show me how! There are people in my life who are so difficult to love. I can barely manage spending time with them. Show me how to express Your love to them that they may be won to You. Amen.

UNSTOPPABLE JOY: ALWAYS REJOICE!

Rejoice in the Lord always; again I will say, rejoice.

PHILIPPIANS 4:4 ESV

Your unstoppable God longs to give you unstoppable joy! "How?" you ask. "When I'm going through seasons of grief or pain? Even then?"

Here's the thing about your heavenly Father's version of joy—it penetrates through the darkness, the depression, the weary days. His joy is able to lift you—not just your emotions, but the whole you. His unstoppable joy is a gift straight from heaven above. And it's one you can ask for more of.

That's right. You can ask for (and receive) more. Daily. In the moment. The Bible says you should rejoice in the Lord always. In fact, God felt so strongly about this decision to live a joy-filled life that He added, "Again I will say, rejoice!"

Why does the Lord care so much about your joy level? Because He knows that His joy is your strength. Without it you're zapped. Add it to the mix and you're good to go!

Lord, I choose joy today. I want Your version of it—the one that lifts every part of me and gives me strength from the inside out! Amen.

COUNT IT ALL JOY

Count it all joy, my brothers, when you meet trials of various kinds.

JAMES 1:2 ESV

Count it *all* joy? All of it? The crummy days? The kids who won't obey? The friends who gossip behind your back? The spouse who forgets to inform you about the big purchase he made? The homeowners' association, after they sent that nasty letter?

Count it *all* joy? The mornings you wake up feeling crummy? The times you catch a glimpse of your chubby physique in the mirror and feel like groaning? Even then?

Here's the truth about God's unstoppable joy—it can turn any situation (even the worst one) into a victory. When you add joy to the mix, it's like dumping sugar into your tea. (If you're from the South, you'll get this analogy!) A little sugar changes everything. A little joy changes everything too.

Once hopeless, you now have hope.

That's the power of joy.

What are the "alls" you're going through today? Count every single one as joy and then watch God turn each one around.

You can do it, Lord! What I cannot accomplish with all my moaning and groaning, You can turn around in an instant with Your unstoppable joy. Enter "all" my situations today, I pray, and do just that! Amen.

YOUR JOY WILL BE FULL

"Until now you have not asked for anything in My name.
Ask and you will receive. Then your joy will be full."

JOHN 16:24 NLV

Maybe you've read verses like Matthew 7:8, 18:19; Luke 11:10; and John 15:7 about receiving whatever you ask for and wonder what they mean. Is God saying we can have *anything* we ask for? Anything at all?

He's not a genie in a bottle. All our wishes won't come true, no matter how much we beg. But we can count on one thing with assurance: He wants us to ask. And this is especially true when it comes to asking for more joy. John 16:24 tells us that we can ask and then receive joy—and not just a little bit! God says that our joy will be full!

If you've ever filled a coffee mug to overflowing, you know what that looks like! "Full" joy means there's no room left over for anything else—like depression or worries. "Full" joy bubbles over onto everyone you meet. And it's yours for the asking. Right here. Right now.

Ask, and you'll receive more joy. Then, as it bubbles up inside you, as it activates your faith, your joy really will spill over onto all of those you come in contact with today!

Lord, thank You for reminding me that I can ask for more. You
stand ready to pour out more joy—for my benefit and for those
around me, that they can see Your good works in my life! Amen.

JOY IS GOOD MEDICINE

A joyful heart is good medicine, but a crushed spirit dries up the bones.
PROVERBS 17:22 ESV

You know what it's like to take medicine when you're sick. You pray it kicks in fast! Sometimes it works, other times not so much. Some meds even cause icky side effects that you hadn't expected. Ugh!

When it comes to God's unstoppable joy, however, there are no negative side effects! It's the best medicine in the world, guaranteed to cure what ails you!

Dealing with heartbreak? Take a hefty dose of joy.

Struggling with pain after the betrayal of a friend? Joy will get you through it.

Battling a physical issue? Does it have you down in the dumps? Ask for joy to lift you above your current circumstances and physical pain.

When your heart is light—filled with unstoppable joy—it's like taking a megadose of vitamin C. Your weary heart springs to life in miraculous fashion and reminds you that hope does exist, even in the pain.

Lord, I love Your kind of medicine! I'll take it every day. Thank You for the reminder that joy is good for my body, mind, and spirit! Amen.

FULLNESS OF JOY

You make known to me the path of life; in your presence there is fullness of joy; at your right hand are pleasures forevermore.

PSALM 16:11 ESV

Have you ever filled a water balloon? If so, then you probably know what it's like to overfill one! Sometimes we squeeze in so much water that the poor balloon simply can't take the strain.

Aren't you glad God's unstoppable joy isn't like that? He pours out more. . .and more. . .and more! We're filled to the tippy-top and He keeps filling. There's no risk of popping our joy bubble when the ointment flowing in is straight from heaven's throne room.

Your unstoppable God longs to fill you up today. Sure, you're facing stuff. Hard stuff. Adding joy to the mix seems impossible. And "fullness" of joy seems more like a pipe dream. But He can do it. Submit yourself, like that little balloon submits itself to the water. Expect to be stretched. Anticipate a change in the shape of things. But don't worry for one minute that you'll pop! Just the opposite will happen, in fact. You will find yourself fully content, fully energized, and ready to face whatever life throws your way. Such is the power of unstoppable joy!

Lord, I'm ready! I'm a little balloon, preparing herself to be stretched to fullness in You. Pour Yourself out, Father! Fill me up, I pray! Amen.

NO THIEF CAN TAKE IT

"So also you have sorrow now, but I will see you again, and your hearts will rejoice, and no one will take your joy from you."

JOHN 16:22 ESV

If you've ever been robbed, you know the fear of living with those icky "What if it happens again?" feelings. They can rob you of your peace of mind, for sure!

The enemy has ninja skills when it comes to zapping you of your peace. He always wants you to think the worst is coming. If you get sick, you're going to die. If you go through financial hardship, you're going to end up poverty stricken. If a friend abandons you, you're a worthless person no one wants to be around. (See how he operates? He's sly!)

Here's some good news for you today, friend! The enemy can't steal God's unstoppable joy. Once the Lord pours it out, the only way to lose it is to hand it over to the enemy. (Resist the temptation!) Hold fast to it. It's yours for the taking. And the transformative power that comes with this joy can be life changing. You'll see—perhaps for the first time—that you have authority over that nagging, lying voice of the enemy. You can look him in the eye and say, "I'm onto you, mister!" You can send him running with just one simple word: *Jesus*!

Lord, thank You for joy that is mine to keep! No thief can take it! I won't let worries or hardship or pain rob me of this precious, holy gift. Amen.

JOY COMES IN THE MORNING

For his anger is but for a moment, and his favor is for a lifetime.
Weeping may tarry for the night, but joy comes with the morning.

PSALM 30:5 ESV

You're not feeling it right now. Sure, folks say, "Just let Jesus take it! Give it to Him! He'll give you joy to get through this." And you believe it way down deep. Still, you're not feeling it. Not yet. Maybe tomorrow.

Here's the truth, friend: you can't conjure up something that is supernatural. The kind of joy infusion you need in moments like that? It's a gift, poured out from God. And He's sensitive to what you're going through. There are very few giggles in a hospital room. His unstoppable joy will look considerably different at a graveside than at a child's first birthday party. It shows up in hugs from family members, notes from friends, or a rainbow in the sky overhead.

If you're not feeling it today, that's okay. The Word of God promises that joy will come in the morning. Even in seasons of deepest grief and pain, your unstoppable God has already begun the process of revealing supernatural joy to get you through.

Lord, I've been through some tough, tough seasons when I haven't always "felt" Your presence. I haven't sensed Your joy. But You've shown up in the smile of a grandchild or the embrace of a friend. Thank You for the reminder that joy always comes. I just have to look for it. Amen.

THIS IS THE DAY!

This is the day that the Lord has made.
Let us be full of joy and be glad in it.

PSALM 118:24 NLV

Deep breath, sister. You want to react. To say something you might regret.

But you don't. You stop, count to ten, and then go on with your day. As you redirect your thoughts, your heart comes into alignment. And though it's difficult, you choose to rejoice and be glad, even on the crummy days when things are coming against you.

Interesting, isn't it, that the Lord gives us the choice. We get to choose to rejoice. . .or not. (No pressure!) Going through a relational struggle? Choose to rejoice. Facing financial woes? Throw a joy party! Battling the flu or tending to a sick child? Offer joy every step of the way.

There's strength in joy! It builds us up from the inside out. It's the strongest supplement you'll ever take! (Truly! It'll cure what ails you!)

This is the day. Choose God's unstoppable joy today, no matter what you're facing.

This is the day, Jesus! I choose joy, in spite of the chaos swirling around me. I won't let distractions keep me from the strength You're offering. It's mine for the taking and I'm so grateful! Amen.

INEXPRESSIBLE

*Though you have not seen him, you love him. Though
you do not now see him, you believe in him and rejoice
with joy that is inexpressible and filled with glory.*

1 PETER 1:8 ESV

Have you ever been so overcome that you simply couldn't express
your feelings? Maybe you stared into the face of a newborn babe and
couldn't put into words what was going on inside your heart. Perhaps
you fell in love or had a major crush on someone but couldn't quite
express your feelings to him. (Ah, romance! Isn't it lovely?)

Joy is often so "otherworldly" in nature that we truly can't cap-
ture it in a turn of phrase. We do our best, but the right words don't
always come! Poets seem to have a knack for it, but the rest of us?
Not so much!

Today's verse is so true! We often rejoice with joy that is "inexpressible and filled with glory." And one day we'll stand in the presence
of God and experience Him in His fullness. Even then the only words
we'll likely be able to express are "Holy, holy, holy is the Lord God
Almighty!" All praise goes back to Him as our hearts are overwhelmed
with our unstoppable God!

*Lord, how I praise You! My heart can't always express what I'm
feeling, but my spirit knows to rejoice! I'm waiting for the day when
I can gather with the saints around the throne to usher up praises.
Until then, I'll do my best with all the words I can gather! Amen.*

HIS JOY, MY STRENGTH

Nehemiah said, "Go and enjoy choice food and sweet drinks, and send some to those who have nothing prepared. This day is holy to our Lord. Do not grieve, for the joy of the LORD is your strength."

NEHEMIAH 8:10 NIV

"Do not grieve, for the joy of the LORD is your strength."

How many times have you stared at this biblical admonition and wondered, *Is that even possible? Can my unstoppable God really give me the kind of joy that sees beyond the pain I'm going through? Is such a thing realistic?*

Friend, this is only possible through the power of the Spirit of God. What you cannot do in the natural, He can do in the Spirit. You can't drum up joy that's needed to get yourself through a season of heartache, but He can pour it out like fresh wine. You can't jump up and down and celebrate your way to a true and lasting victory, but He can supernaturally give you strength to get there. In other words, it's on Him. It's His joy that's your strength, not your own.

Read that again. *It's His joy, not your own.* You can "try" to be happy, but it will accomplish nothing. Instead, pray for a supernatural infusion. One sip of that joy and you'll have hope as never before!

Lord, I get it. I can't conjure up joy. It's not up to me! It's Your joy I'm seeking, Lord. And I trust You to pour it out, my unstoppable God!

UNSTOPPABLE PEACE

*"You keep him in perfect peace whose mind
is stayed on you, because he trusts in you."*
ISAIAH 26:3 ESV

Your unstoppable God wants to pour out unstoppable peace. On those days when you're ready to walk away from your job. In those moments when you want to hide in the bathroom to get away from your kids. During those instances on the highway where the guy in the next car is driving like a maniac. Even then God's peace is unstoppable. It will chase you down. It won't give you the option to say no.

You can open yourself up to God's peace flow by getting out of your own head. Calm your thoughts. Give them to Him. Discard what the Bible calls "vain imaginings" (irrational fears that crop up when hard times hit). The enemy would love to distract you with those time zappers. God, on the other hand? He knows better. His peace is perfect and it's Johnny-on-the-spot. It works in a hurry!

Think about that word *perfect*. God's peace lacks nothing. It's a complete game changer. So keep your thoughts—your mind and your heart—on Him. When you place your trust in the Creator of all, supernatural peace is yours for the taking.

*Thank You, Jesus, for giving me peace. Redirect my thoughts.
I don't want to focus on my worries and fears. I give those to You,
my unstoppable God, and anticipate a peaceful result. Amen.*

THOSE WONDERFUL PEACEMAKERS

"Blessed are the peacemakers, for they will be called children of God."
MATTHEW 5:9 NIV

There are peacekeepers, and then there are peacemakers. Peacekeepers hate turmoil and often refuse to contradict someone for fear of trouble erupting. Peacemakers do the hard thing: confront when necessary so that there can be true peace in the end.

Whether you're a peacekeeper or a peacemaker, no doubt you long for true and lasting peace—between friends, in romantic relationships, with your kids and grandkids. That's why the peacemakers of this world, the ones who are willing to do the hard work, need to be honored! They aren't in it to throw a bandage on a problem. No, they're willing to do the deep therapeutic work to make sure the core of the problem is resolved.

Your unstoppable God loves peacemaking. It's not easy to confront. It's not easy to speak hard truth in love. But if the ultimate end goal is peace, then it's always worth it.

> *I'll admit it, Lord—I don't always have the courage to be*
> *a true peacemaker. I'm most often a peacekeeper, someone*
> *who tucks her tail between her legs and quietly shuts down.*
> *But You're teaching me how to be brave. As the world*
> *grows darker, may my light grow brighter, I pray! Amen.*

AS IT DEPENDS ON YOU

If possible, so far as it depends on you, live peaceably with all.
ROMANS 12:18 ESV

Aren't you glad the world isn't depending on you to fix all the major woes facing humankind today? Talk about an impossible situation to find yourself in! You don't have the kind of know-how needed to bring about world peace or to solve issues like pandemics.

That's not to say you have no role to play. Your unstoppable God has a major role for you! And yes, it will affect the outcome of many situations and, in its own right, bring about peace for yourself and your inner circle.

You have the power to effect change with those you love by living at peace with all. When your friend picks a fight. When your husband gets on your last nerve. When the kids have tried your patience for the last time. As it depends on you (and it does in those instances), you can choose to live at peace.

It won't be easy. In fact, choosing peace in the middle of turmoil can feel downright impossible. But you must choose it anyway. If every believer would effect change in his or her circle, imagine how many millions of healed/whole circles there would be across the globe!

Lord, I'll do my best. It won't be easy, but I'll try to live at peace with everyone You've placed in my circle. Help me, I pray. Amen.

NOT AS THE WORLD GIVES

"Peace I leave with you; my peace I give you. I do not give to you as the world gives. Do not let your hearts be troubled and do not be afraid."

JOHN 14:27 NIV

"Go get a massage!" "Drink some chamomile tea." "Take a nap, girl!"

Good advice, all the way around, especially when you're stressed! The world offers all sorts of tips and suggestions for overtaxed folks. "Talk to a therapist." "Eat a healthy diet." "Get a good night's sleep." The list of suggestions goes on and on.

There's nothing wrong with the world's way of dealing with turmoil and anxiety, but God has a better way! Today's scripture clues us in: "I do not give to you as the world gives."

Whoa. God is giving us something better than a massage? Something more calming than a cup of chamomile? Yes, He's offering us true and lasting peace. Unlike a massage, the effects won't wear off in a hurry. (Also, it's free!) Supernatural, unstoppable peace can be yours for the asking. So when you're headed to the bedroom for that much-needed nap, don't forget to pause to ask for God's solution to the problem. Instead of a troubled heart, instead of fear, you can tuck yourself into bed assured of the fact that your unstoppable God will wrap you in a blanket of peace that will stand the test of time.

Lord, thank You for Your kind of peace! It's better than anything the world has to offer. Amen.

RULING IN YOUR HEART

And let the peace of Christ rule in your hearts, to which indeed you were called in one body. And be thankful.

COLOSSIANS 3:15 ESV

What sits on the throne of your heart? Many parents would say, "My kids!" Those who love their career might say, "My job!" Of course, most believers would be quick to say, "Jesus, of course!" (Hint: right answer!)

Whoever (or whatever) sits on the throne of your heart determines both your internal and external thermometer. How "hot" (worked up) you get will be ruled by whatever you've placed in control of your heart.

That's why it's so important to acknowledge the role that Jesus intends for His supernatural peace to play. When you allow it to "rule" in your heart (to call the shots) the temperature goes *way* down. This is helpful, not just for your own personal peace level, but as an ointment for the relationships you're trying to maintain. If we're called to be one body (and we are), then the rulership of peace is more important than ever. Lose it, and chaos results! Keep it in its rightful place, and even the most difficult situations are doable.

Lord, I invite You to rule and reign in my heart with peace leading the way! I don't want to blow steam like a teakettle. For my sake and for theirs, I want to remain cool, calm, and collected. This can only happen if I let You fully reign in my heart. Amen.

DWELLING IN SAFETY

In peace I will lie down and sleep, for you alone, LORD, make me dwell in safety.

PSALM 4:8 NIV

It's tough to sleep at night if you have the constant niggling fear that a burglar is outside your door! You'll toss and turn all night, imagining the scenarios.

Your unstoppable God wants to remind you that you can rest easy with Him on the job. He will make you dwell in safety. The kind of peace He offers is the *"Please just let me handle this, kiddo"* type. It only works if you take a hands-off approach and let Him actually take control.

Releasing control isn't easy, for sure. We're taught to take charge of our lives. And to a certain extent, we should! But when it comes to trusting your Creator to take care of you? Well, you can certainly rest easy knowing He never sleeps or slumbers! He's wide awake all night long, ready to fight on your behalf if necessary! So, catch some z's, girl! God is on the job!

Lord, I can dwell in safety with You in control. You're unstoppable in Your quest to bring peace to my soul, even when I'm sleeping. I'll pass the reins to You, Father, and trust You for a favorable outcome. Amen.

SET YOUR MIND ON THE SPIRIT

For to set the mind on the flesh is death, but to
set the mind on the Spirit is life and peace.

ROMANS 8:6 ESV

What are you thinking about right now? At this very moment. What's on your mind? What is consuming your thoughts? If you're like most twenty-first-century Christians, you are troubled by many things—finances. Job. Family issues. Relational struggles. On and on the list goes. And these things can take up a huge chunk of real estate in your head and heart. In fact, they can become consuming.

God has a different way for you to live! He doesn't want you to be consumed by the cares of life. He wants to elevate your thinking, to lift your thoughts above all of that. This is only possible when you set your mind on the Spirit.

How do you do that? In the moment, as the cares wrap their tendrils around your heart, stop and pray. Refocus. Instead of thinking of your own limitations, what you can't accomplish in the flesh, turn your eyes upon Jesus. Think about what He can do through the power of His Spirit. Once you realize your supernatural, unstoppable God is on the job, all those worries will cease. He's got this, girl. He's got this.

Whew! You've got this, Lord. I'll set my mind on
things above. What I can't handle, You can! Amen.

IN PURSUIT OF PEACE

*"Turn away from evil and do good. Search
for peace, and work to maintain it."*

1 PETER 3:11 NLT

Have you ever played hide-and-seek? It's fun when you're the one doing the hiding. You're sure that "seeker" will never find you. You've chosen your hiding spot well! Only that person usually does find you and your hopes are dashed. Then it's your turn to do the seeking.

When it comes to God's unstoppable peace, there's a never-ending game of hide-and-seek going on. Peace is there, but you have to search it out. You have to look for it. (Hint: it's not always easy to find!) To locate it, you have to be as focused as that "seeker" in the game you played. You have to be single minded. Driven. Determined.

To find peace, you must turn away from distractions. Temptations. Evil. Poor choices. You have to do the right thing. (This is the hard part sometimes!) But when you're hyperfocused on the goal, you'll locate peace every single time!

*Lord, I won't give up! I'll be like a hunter going after my game! I won't
stop until peace is located. Thanks for reminding me that I must turn
away from wickedness and pursue peace with all diligence. Amen.*

PEACE THROUGH CHRIST

Therefore, since we have been justified by faith, we have
peace with God through our Lord Jesus Christ.

ROMANS 5:1 ESV

Ah, love! You've found "the one." He makes you feel so good!

Until he doesn't. Then you're ready to cry foul! How could this perfect-for-you-person let you down like that? How could he take your fragile heart and trample on it? (Hint: he's human!)

If you're looking for someone who will never let you down, who really *will* bring lasting peace, then you'll find Him only in the person of Jesus Christ. He has justified us by faith (made us "just as if" we had never sinned). And because of this, His peace can take ownership of our hearts.

This infusion of supernatural peace can only come for the one who acknowledges Jesus as Lord and Savior of all. The decision to follow Him results in a life of peace, joy, faith, and blessing. When you find "the One," He really *does* make you feel good. And (bonus!) He won't ever break your heart. You can take that promise to the bank.

Lord, thank You for the gift of Your Son! I've found the One
my heart was longing for. And His unstoppable love has
graced me with a thousand gifts, including supernatural,
inexplicable peace! How I praise You! Amen.

PEACE THAT PASSES
ALL UNDERSTANDING

*The peace of God, which surpasses all understanding,
will guard your hearts and your minds in Christ Jesus.*

PHILIPPIANS 4:7 ESV

Think of your favorite subject in school. If you were, say, a math kid, then you probably loved solving equations. The longer and more complicated, the better. (Hey, there's nothing like a challenge to put your imagination to work!)

Solving problems is so satisfying, isn't it? But not every problem in life has a solution. People get sick and pass away. Marriages end in divorce. Friends get angry and walk away from relationships. There's no class to get you ready for this kind of schooling. It's hard knocks all the way.

Fortunately, the believer is offered a special gift that makes these valleys a bit easier to navigate. Jesus offers us peace that surpasses all understanding. You don't have to know the answer. You don't have to understand why he left or why she blew up at you like she did. Even if you never solve the problem, peace can guard your heart and your mind as you tromp through the muddy patches.

*Lord, I'm not the best problem solver. I'll leave the
really hard ones to You! You are my unstoppable God,
the One who knows all the answers to all of life's
questions. I know I can trust You, Father! Amen.*

UNSTOPPABLE PATIENCE

Rejoice in hope, be patient in tribulation, be constant in prayer.
ROMANS 12:12 ESV

"Be patient, dear! Be patient!" No doubt you heard those words a lot growing up! Patience can seem like one of those elusive things you strive for but never actually reach.

Fortunately, your unstoppable God stands ready to offer you more. And more. And more. For sure, it's true what they say: if you pray for patience, you'll surely find a reason to need it. But isn't that the point, really? Jesus led by example, didn't He? He taught us to rejoice in hope (remember the story of Lazarus being raised from the dead?), to be patient in tribulation (remember the time He healed the woman with the issue of blood?), and to be constant in prayer (as He was, in the garden when His disciples dozed off and left Him alone).

Unstoppable patience really can be yours. All you have to do is follow the lead of your Savior. He's ready, willing, and able to show you how to live a patient, consistent life.

I'll look to You, Jesus! You're the One leading and guiding me. Thank You for being patient with me. Please help me exhibit that same patience toward others! Amen.

DON'T GIVE UP!

So let's not get tired of doing what is good. At just the right time we will reap a harvest of blessing if we don't give up.

GALATIANS 6:9 NLT

You're weary. You've reached the breaking point. You couldn't take another step forward even if you had to.

And yet you have to. Life doesn't give you any other choice. There are still kids to be fed, dishes to be washed, pets to be cleaned up after. There's that work situation you can't avoid, that pesky neighbor who won't stop complaining about your lawn, or maybe that scale with its *You need to drop a few pounds!* message.

Life is hard. You'll reach a thousand jumping-off points where you say, "Nope. I'm done. Put a fork in me." The temptation to climb into bed and pull the covers over your head will be overwhelming.

It's okay to give in for a minute. Or a few hours. But don't give up for good! Don't grow weary in doing good. Your unstoppable God is here to remind you today that you will reap a reward—if you don't give up!

Lord, I won't give up. I'll keep putting one foot in front of the other. Thank You, my unstoppable God, for reminding me that I can be unstoppable as well. Amen.

BEAR WITH ONE ANOTHER

With all humility and gentleness, with patience,
[bear] with one another in love.
EPHESIANS 4:2 ESV

Your unstoppable God has been very patient with you. (This might be a good opportunity to pause and think of the many, many times He exhibited unstoppable patience on your behalf. You might also offer up a prayer of thanks.)

Now God is asking you to be unstoppable in your patience with others. Ouch. That's harder! You're not God, after all. You're only human.

Yes, you're a human who is created in the image and likeness of a holy God. And He has given you all the tools you'll need to offer humility, gentleness, and patience to others as you navigate your way through the rough patches. (Hint: there will be plenty of rough patches to prove this out!)

Bear with one another. Think about those words. To bear means to carry. It might get weighty. It might get hard. But in the hard times, there's one word that helps you patiently navigate. That word is *love*. Bear in love. It might not be easy, but it's God's way.

> *Lord, I'll do my best to bear with others and to be more*
> *patient, but I will need Your help! Give me the humility*
> *and gentleness needed to get the job done, I pray. Amen.*

RENEWED STRENGTH

*Those who trust in the LORD will find new strength.
They will soar high on wings like eagles. They will run
and not grow weary. They will walk and not faint.*

ISAIAH 40:31 NLT

You purchased those rechargeable batteries for a reason. It's easier to plug them in and give them extra juice than to start over with new, expensive batteries.

This recharging process spills over into your life, just as it does with your batteries. You will go through seasons of refreshing and recharging. During these seasons, you'll get the energy (and yes, patience!) you need to keep going, to keep dealing with life's many complicated issues.

There's a lovely promise in today's verse. When you pause to wait on God during these rough patches, He renews your strength. (He recharges your proverbial battery.) Then, once you're recharged, you're filled with enough *Zap! Zam! Zow!* to take off flying! You'll run and not be weary. You'll walk and not faint. God's supernatural, unstoppable power will energize you for the tasks ahead!

*Thank You, my unstoppable God, for giving me the boost I need
to keep going! You keep my batteries charged and ready for use!
How grateful I am for that supernatural energy. Amen.*

DON'T FRET

Be still before the LORD and wait patiently for him;
fret not yourself over the one who prospers in his
way, over the man who carries out evil devices!

PSALM 37:7 ESV

It's one thing to say, "Hey, be patient!" It's another altogether to add, "And while you're at it, don't fret." Um. Don't fret? Is that really possible?

Here's the thing about your unstoppable God: in one split second He can do what you can't do in years of trying. Talk about remarkable! His powers are supernatural and so far above yours. When you think about it that way, does it put things in perspective?

Yes, you want to fret. Anxiety keeps you knotted up on the inside, especially when evil people seem to prosper all around you. (What's up with that?)

But God. . .

Don't you love those words? He can squelch the fears inside you while simultaneously dealing with the evil in this crazy world. He's big enough and strong enough to handle it all. So, take a deep breath. Relax. You might be on hold at the moment, but God will have His way—and His say.

Lord, while I'm waiting I'll do my best to rid myself of anxiety. Take this fretful heart, I pray, and bring peace in the middle of life's storms. Amen.

THE END OF A THING

Finishing is better than starting. Patience is better than pride.
ECCLESIASTES 7:8 NLT

Have you ever reached the "giving-up" point? Maybe a relationship turned sour and you felt it couldn't bounce back. Or perhaps you went through a financial crisis and saw no upbeat resolution in sight.

It's easy to throw in the towel when you can't see the end of a thing. Oh, but if you could, perhaps you would hang on a bit longer! If you knew that your unstoppable God was going to completely turn that relationship around, would you hang on? If you realized ahead of time that He was going to provide a miracle to see you through the lean seasons, would you trust Him while waiting?

God sees it all—beginning, middle, and end. All He asks of us is that we trust Him in the middle. It's not easy, but when you offer Him a pliable heart, one willing to bend with the seasons, He will show off big in the end! (And what joy to hang on for the long haul!)

Lord, I can't see the end of my story. I can't even see how today will conclude. But this one thing I know: I can trust You. You have a plan for my days and have mapped out some exciting experiences ahead. I know I can count on You, my unstoppable God! Until I see the end, give me supernatural patience. Amen.

SLOW TO ANGER

*Know this, my beloved brothers: let every person
be quick to hear, slow to speak, slow to anger.*

JAMES 1:19 ESV

"Be quick to hear, slow to speak, slow to anger."

Whoa. No doubt you could write an entire sermon just on those few words. If you're like most people, you're slow to hear, quick to speak, and you rush forward with anger when things don't go your way. (Isn't it interesting that God asks us to demonstrate the very opposite spirit than what comes naturally to us?)

Be slow to anger. Even when you're justified. Even when the other person is wrong, wrong, wrong. Be quick to hear. Even when the other person makes no sense and you're dying to get your point out there.

These things might seem impossible, but your unstoppable God can give you the patience required. No matter where you are today, no matter what struggles you're facing, know that your unstoppable heavenly Father wants to show you how to live in this brave, new way.

*It won't come naturally, Lord! I want to spout off, to speak my mind
with my temper leading the way! But You're showing me another
option, and it's one I must take. Thank You for the reminder that
I can become more like You if I'll just take a deep breath! Amen.*

CHARACTER IS BEING PRODUCED

*When we have learned not to give up, it shows we have stood
the test. When we have stood the test, it gives us hope.*

ROMANS 5:4 NLV

You wonder if it's worth it. All this waiting. All this agony. Will there
be a payoff in the end?

Here's the great thing about how your unstoppable God works:
while you're waiting, He's busy building character. You won't come
out of this the same way you went into it. You'll be a different person.
Your heart will be changed, yes, but so will your thoughts. And your
actions. Possibly even your motivations.

God is growing you. He's stretching you. And though you're in a
season that requires great patience, He's also teaching you that you're
capable of waiting. And then waiting some more.

Endurance produces character. Character produces hope. You
can have hope today because God is right there pouring out His
unstoppable patience to get you through.

*Lord, You're changing me. I sense it. I feel it. And while I'm
waiting, I know I can count on You to do marvelous things
inside me. I offer myself as putty in Your hands—pliable.
Willing. Ready to be changed from the inside out. Amen.*

GOOD SOIL

*"As for that in the good soil, they are those who, hearing the word,
hold it fast in an honest and good heart, and bear fruit with patience."*

LUKE 8:15 ESV

You're in a waiting season, and it's making you antsy. You wish you could put this behind you, move on toward the goal. But you can't. You're stuck, at least for now. And you wonder if God sees or knows your pain.

Meanwhile, He's busy pouring out message after message—through His Word, even through the voices of others who are trying to minister to you. Are those messages falling on good soil? Are you receptive to them, or has your impatience made it impossible for hope to slip through?

Your unstoppable God wants to remind you today that He's still speaking. Some days He whispers to your heart; other days He shouts in your ear (possibly through a friend or social media post). But He never stops trying. The soil of your heart needs to remain good so that you're receptive to His Word.

Hear it. Believe it. Hold fast to it. Then, in due season, you will bear fruit with much patience. Hang in there, girl. Good news is coming.

*Lord, I get it. My impatience makes me deaf to Your
cries. I want to have good soil, even while I'm waiting.
Open my ears and soften my heart, I pray. Amen.*

PERSUASIVE PATIENCE

*When one is slow to anger, a ruler may be
won over. A gentle tongue will break a bone.*

PROVERBS 25:15 NLV

Have you ever considered the notion that your patience could be considered persuasive? It's true! When you hold out hope, even in hopeless times, people are watching. They're wondering why you keep going against the odds. When you're facing an obstacle but don't give up, they're paying attention. Waiting to see how you'll handle yourself.

People are noticing you. The way you do what you say you'll do. The way you hang on, even when it makes no sense. The kind, upbeat words you speak, even in the middle of the storms. They're noticing and they care. Your life choices are affecting others. They want what you have. And you can show them how to obtain it by following hard after your unstoppable God, even when the chips are down! So, keep on keeping on, girl! Don't stop.

*Lord, I want to be a good witness for You, even in the waiting
seasons. May my light shine bright as I offer hope for the hopeless.
May every action on my part lead them straight to You, Jesus! Amen.*

UNSTOPPABLE KINDNESS

Be kind to one another, tenderhearted, forgiving
one another, as God in Christ forgave you.

EPHESIANS 4:32 ESV

Your unstoppable God is pouring out unstoppable kindness, even when you don't deserve it. He keeps giving and giving and giving some more, even when you give up. He keeps loving you through the hard patches, even after you've sworn Him off. He simply won't stop.

Through His immeasurable kindness, Jesus is teaching you how to live. And He's hoping you'll catch on sooner rather than later. Why? Because He longs for that same kindness to be a part of your lifestyle! When you learn to pour out unstoppable kindness, the world around you is changed for the better. And it's addictive! Before long, those you are kind to will do the same for others. And so on. And so on.

So be kind to all. Be tenderhearted, even when you don't feel like it. Forgive, even when it makes no sense. Why? Because your kindhearted heavenly Father has done the same for you.

I get it, Lord! You're chasing me down with Your kindness and hoping
I'll do the same for others. It's not always easy, but this is one lesson
I hope to learn and pass on—for the good of humanity! Amen.

A BENEFIT TO ALL

A man who is kind benefits himself, but a cruel man hurts himself.
PROVERBS 11:17 ESV

Who are you benefiting when you show unstoppable kindness the way God shows it to you? Yourself? Sure, it's always self-benefiting to be kind to others. It makes you feel good on the inside. Of course, it's also a joy to others when they're treated with kindness. (Think of how you feel when others have lavished it on you.)

Now look at the reverse: when you're cruel to others, when you withhold kindness, you're not just hurting them; you're hurting yourself. Ultimately, you're wounding your own heart. Stepping away from the example Christ set for you breaks His heart and eventually your own. He longs for you to be a visible demonstration of His love to others no matter what. Step away from that and everyone gets hurt.

It's not always easy to do the right thing. That's true. It might even feel impossible at times. But as much as it is possible with you, live peacefully, with kindness leading the way.

> *Lord, I want to be known as one who is kind to others. I know that ultimately my own heart will be softened and pliable as I pour out Your unstoppable kindness on others. I need Your help to accomplish this, Father! Amen.*

PUT IT ON

As God's chosen people, holy and dearly loved, clothe yourselves
with compassion, kindness, humility, gentleness and patience.

COLOSSIANS 3:12 NIV

If you're like most women, you get dressed in a hurry each morning. No doubt you're rushing to get the kids to school or to head to work. There's a lot to be done in a short period of time. (And let's admit it—mornings are tough!)

God wants you to put on kindness each day. Add it to your wardrobe in much the same way you'd put on a blouse or a pair of earrings. When you forget to put on kindness, you limit the extent to which God can use you. It's true! When you're unwilling to be kind to others, you're not shining your light as He longs for you to.

Turn on that light, girl! Keep it shining brightly by adorning yourself with kindness. You're His chosen child—holy and beloved—and He wants your heart to be compassionate, humble, meek, and patient.

Lord, I'll admit it—I don't always dress myself in humility and
kindness each day. I head off to work frantic, worried, upset.
I'm not thinking of others the way You want me to. May I be a
reflection of You, Jesus, in the way I treat others every day. Amen.

THE TEACHING OF KINDNESS

She opens her mouth with wisdom, and the
teaching of kindness is on her tongue.
PROVERBS 31:26 ESV

Is the teaching of kindness on your tongue? (Tough question, right?) Perhaps you've never considered yourself a teacher, one way or the other. Maybe you don't think about the fact that others are watching and listening to the way you talk to your children, your friends, or your spouse. But they are. They are looking to you, one of God's beloved, as an example, a representation of Him. And they're hoping to find kindness on your tongue.

This might be a good day to ask the Lord to baptize your tongue with kindness. (Hey, He can do it!) When you open your mouth, may only kindness slip out! May it be the first thing on the tip of your tongue. Not a sharp word. Not a criticism. Not gossip. Just pure, unstoppable kindness—the same kindness the Lord has offered you time and time again. What a wonderful world this would be if everyone lived this way!

Lord, baptize my tongue with kindness! I want to speak as You
speak, love as You love! Thank You, my unstoppable God, for the
kindness You've bestowed on me through the years! Amen.

LOVE IS KIND

Love is patient and kind; love does not envy or boast; it is not arrogant or rude. It does not insist on its own way; it is not irritable or resentful; it does not rejoice at wrongdoing, but rejoices with the truth. Love bears all things, believes all things, hopes all things, endures all things.

1 CORINTHIANS 13:4–7 ESV

"Hey, I'm a loving person!" you say. And then you bite someone's head off. "I'm kind to others!" you add and then cut someone off in traffic.

So, are you really who you say you are, woman of God? Are you living out the message you're proclaiming with your lips, or do your actions speak louder than words? Are those hard questions for you to answer?

The world is paying attention, not just to your words, but to your life. They're watching how you speak to your coworkers. How you treat that waitress who got your order wrong. How you talk to that cranky neighbor who's grating on your nerves. They're watching, and they might also be wondering why your actions don't line up with your verbal message. Ouch!

It's not too late to turn things around! Your unstoppable God can show you how to match your lips to your life when you submit to Him. May every message be a kind message!

Lord, I want to be a reflection of You—not just with what I say but in how I live. May I never wound or hurt others. May I only shine a light of kindness wherever I go! Amen.

NO EVIL FOR EVIL, PLEASE!

Do not repay evil with evil or insult with insult.
On the contrary, repay evil with blessing, because to
this you were called so that you may inherit a blessing.

1 PETER 3:9 NIV

God has a "no evil for evil" policy. He's hoping you will respond kindly, even when wounded by others.

What does this look like? Say someone smarts off to you—perhaps at work. You want to snap back. But you don't. Or someone treats you unkindly and you're tempted to get even by gossiping to others about what they've done. But you choose a different path. You forgive. You keep moving forward with the friendship, doing all you can to love in spite of the injury.

The Lord longs for His kids to have an unstoppable love for others, one that demonstrates kindness, even in difficult situations. And this "no evil for evil" lifestyle can be transformative, not just for those you're kind to, but also to yourself. It's a refreshing way to live!

Bless others. You were called to do so. Bless; don't curse. Love; don't hate. In doing so, you too will obtain a blessing. That's how our unstoppable God works!

Lord, I get it. When I'm good to others, I reap the benefits. When I
bless, I receive a blessing. I don't want to fall short in this area, Father!
Help me to treat others kindly even when I don't feel like it! Amen.

THE SEVERITY OF GOD

Note then the kindness and the severity of God: severity toward those who have fallen, but God's kindness to you, provided you continue in his kindness. Otherwise you too will be cut off.

ROMANS 11:22 ESV

It might seem a bit ironic to talk about the severity of God and the kindness of God in the same sentence. Those two thoughts seem to be opposites. They are, in fact, compatible. It's the kindness of God that leads to repentance. Repentance saves us from His severity.

Those who accept His kindness and turn toward Him can receive healing. Life. Restoration. For those who choose to turn away from Him, there is only pain and suffering. He can't—and won't—protect them from themselves if they so willingly neglect His kindness.

Your unstoppable God wants you to accept His kindness, to turn back to Him, and to repent when you've fallen away. When you lead by example, the world will pay attention. They will be drawn to His kindness too.

Lord, thank You for drawing me back, time and time again! I would much rather accept Your kindness than to experience Your severity as a result of my stubbornness! This is my prayer for those I love too. May they come to know You for Your kindness as well, I pray. Amen.

THE RICHES OF HIS KINDNESS

Don't you see how wonderfully kind, tolerant, and patient
God is with you? Does this mean nothing to you? Can't you
see that his kindness is intended to turn you from your sin?

ROMANS 2:4 NLT

Imagine you lived in a palace alongside the king of the land. He owned every good thing, and all of it could be yours for the asking. (Wow! Can you imagine?) What would you ask for first? (It's fun to think about, isn't it?)

Here's the coolest thing about your unstoppable God: He really is the King—of everything! And He owns the cattle on a thousand hills. He loves you so much that He wants to pour out His riches on you. So you really can come to Him with your requests.

God's kindness has a wonderful end result, by the way. When He pours it out, it's always meant to lead you straight back to Him. So instead of focusing on yourself first—your wants, your wishes, your needs—He somehow manages to teach you that it's all about Him, not you. What a wonderful, unstoppable King we serve!

Lord, I'm so grateful that You've told me to ask! You have
unsearchable riches available at my disposal. And You're willing
to give them, not so that my storehouse can be full, but so that I'll
fall deeper in love with You. I'm grateful You love me so! Amen.

WHAT THE LORD REQUIRES OF YOU

He has told you, O man, what is good; and what does the LORD require of you but to do justice, and to love kindness, and to walk humbly with your God?

MICAH 6:8 ESV

God is good. God is kind. And He longs for you to follow His lead, sharing that same goodness and kindness with the world around you. Best of all, God has a plan—a formula, if you will—for how you can accomplish those things. You'll find that formula in today's verse: *Do justice. Treat all people fairly. Do right by them. Think as much of others as you think of yourself.*

Love kindness. It's not enough to love people. You actually have to love the act of kindness as well. You need to adopt it as a lifestyle. It will radically change how you live and how you treat others.

Finally, this verse encourages you to walk humbly with your God. Acknowledge that His way is better. Become more like Him. Ask for His thoughts, His heart for others. He will surely give it!

God's formula will lead to the best possible outcome no matter what you're facing.

Lord, I thank You for giving me a strategy to love others. I want to follow Your lead, Father! Amen.

ONLY FOR BUILDING UP

Let no corrupting talk come out of your mouths,
but only such as is good for building up, as fits the
occasion, that it may give grace to those who hear.

EPHESIANS 4:29 ESV

Oh, how we love to let those harsh words fly when we're upset. We spew them out like venom on unsuspecting loved ones and friends. Ouch. These moments, which we usually live to regret, should happen less frequently the longer we walk with God.

His plan? If we followed God's plan, we would give up corrupt talk altogether. We would speak only words meant to build others up. Think about that for a moment: How would your speech change if you could say only positive things? That's a goal we should strive for. We can become more like Him if we give up corrupt talk and adopt kindness in its place.

Give grace. Love. Speak gracious words meant to uplift. When you live like this, you're a direct reflection of your unstoppable God!

Lord, thank You for the reminder that I can
(and should) give up corrupt speech. I'm going to do
my best to be more like You in this way, Jesus! Amen.

UNSTOPPABLE GOODNESS

Surely your goodness and love will follow me all the days of my life, and I will dwell in the house of the LORD forever.

PSALM 23:6 NIV

The goodness of God is chasing you down at this very moment. It's true! He has been nothing but good to you through the years. Even when you didn't deserve it. (Especially when you didn't deserve it!) And He longs for this same unstoppable goodness to become a lifestyle for you too.

Why, you ask? When goodness follows you all the days of your life, you dwell in safety. There's no safer place to dwell than in the goodness of God!

Also, goodness leads to repentance. When you're good to others, you lead by example! Good people make for good people. Others will long for the same "good" lifestyle you enjoy when you lead this way.

So let goodness do its work—in your life and in your heart. Then you will learn to treat others with unstoppable goodness as well.

Lord, I'm so grateful for Your goodness. It has led me to repentance many times over! Thank You for the safety Your goodness provides. Please help me to demonstrate this lifestyle to others, I pray. Amen.

TASTE AND SEE!

Oh, taste and see that the LORD is good!
Blessed is the man who takes refuge in him!

PSALM 34:8 ESV

Remember as a kid how you turned your nose up at certain foods your mom would fix? No way did you want that broccoli! Or those brussels sprouts. Or that cauliflower. Before even tasting those veggies, you proclaimed them nasty. A few bites, however, eventually convinced you otherwise. Now that you're fully grown, you actually love them!

That's how it is with the goodness of God. Many people say, "He's not a good God. If He is, then why does He allow so many bad things to happen in the world?" They don't understand the fallen state of man, for sure!

Oh, if only they would taste God's goodness, they would be convinced! He wants only good for His kids. God's unstoppable goodness is available for all—rich, poor, young, old. It's meant for every race, every creed, every nation!

God is good. End of story. And once your eyes are finally opened to that knowledge, they'll never be closed again!

Thank You, my precious, good Creator! I've tasted and seen
for myself that Your goodness is leaps and bounds above
anything else I've ever experienced. Thank You, thank You
for pouring out Your goodness on us, Your kids. Amen.

ABUNDANT GOODNESS

Oh, how abundant is your goodness, which you have stored
up for those who fear you and worked for those who take
refuge in you, in the sight of the children of mankind!

PSALM 31:19 ESV

God isn't just a "little bit" good. He's abundantly good! His goodness
goes above and beyond anything we could ask or think. Even now
He's cooking up great things for you. (Hey, He just can't quit! He
adores you, girl!)

No matter how good you are to the children in your life, you'll
never come close to the kind of goodness we're talking about here!
God has "stored up" good things for you. Wow. Think about that.
There's a proverbial storage room with your name on it. Inside are all
sorts of heavenly wonders just for you! Your unstoppably good Father
delights in blessing you. How fun is that?

Take delight in Him. Take refuge in Him. Trust in Him. This
holy, good God will guide and protect you all the days of your life if
you will keep your focus on Him.

Oh, how abundant is His goodness!

Thank You, my unstoppable God! You're pouring out Your goodness
on me—far beyond anything I could imagine. I do nothing to
deserve it, but that doesn't stop You. How grateful I am! Amen.

THE LAND OF THE LIVING

I believe that I shall look upon the goodness
of the LORD in the land of the living!

PSALM 27:13 ESV

These are scary times we're living in. Christians are losing their freedoms in a variety of ways. Pandemics are sweeping the globe. People of faith are being put to death for their faith. Truly, the negative stuff could get overwhelming if you stopped to think about it all at once.

That said, God is still good! He's moving, even now, in the hearts of the ones who are being persecuted. Giving peace. Giving hope. He never stops pouring Himself out on behalf of those He loves.

Today's verse brings such hope in troubled times! We have this promise from God that we can look upon His goodness in the land of the living. While we are here on planet Earth, while we're still breathing, hoping, and praying for the kingdom to come, we can have hope. May we keep Him alive in our hearts, in our speech, and in our actions!

Lord, You're very much alive, no matter how hard the world
tries to shut You down. While there is breath in my lungs, I
will proclaim Your goodness, my unstoppable God! Amen.

EVERY GOOD GIFT IS FROM GOD

*Every good gift and every perfect gift is from above,
coming down from the Father of lights, with whom
there is no variation or shadow due to change.*

JAMES 1:17 ESV

Don't you love Christmas? Gift giving can be so much fun! No doubt you enjoy wrapping up the presents you've purchased with decorative paper and topping them off with ribbons and bows. You take great care with the process. Why? Because it feels really good to bless others.

Now think about all the gifts you've received over the years from your unstoppable God. He's supplied all your needs. Blessed you with amazing relationships. Given you a place to live, food to eat, and health to enjoy it all.

Every good and perfect gift you've ever received (even better than those Christmas gifts) comes from Him. He doesn't know how to give a bad gift! So, remember to pause to thank Him. It's the goodness of God reflected in the blessings He's poured out on you!

*Lord, thank You for pouring out so many precious gifts.
You've blessed me abundantly. You've tenderly wrapped up
these offerings with proverbial ribbons and bows. How
You love me, Lord! And how I love You too! Amen.*

WHEN YOU'RE IN TROUBLE

The LORD is good, a refuge in times of trouble.
He cares for those who trust in him.

NAHUM 1:7 NIV

Where do you run when you're in trouble? If you're like most people, you search out a good friend or maybe a family member to confide in. Still others search for a pastor or counselor to offer advice. These are all good options, especially if your struggles are impossible to deal with on your own.

Yes, going to trusted advisers is great, but take another look at today's verse. Your unstoppable God loves it when you seek *Him* out in the day of trouble. He's your Stronghold, after all. He's your Hiding Place, a safety net where you can take refuge. Because He's a good God, He's ready to hide you under His wing, to protect you when you're going through a rough season. Talk about feeling safe!

He's not just good in the day of trouble, but on good days too! Still your heavenly Father is hopeful you'll run to Him the next time you need a listening ear. He's the best possible help in times of need.

Lord, may I run first to You! I don't want to be guilty of
forgetting You when things get tough. (You never forget
me, after all!) Thanks for being my Safe Place! Amen.

ARE GOOD. DO GOOD.

You are good and do good; teach me your statutes.

PSALM 119:68 ESV

Have you ever heard someone say, "She's a really good person"? What do you think they mean when they say that? How do you know if someone is good or not?

We find a hint in today's verse, which focuses on the attributes of our heavenly Father: "You *are* good and *do* good." We know that God is good to us because, well, He's good to us. We see it in His actions. We feel it in how He tenderly treats us, even when we go astray.

The same is true with God's people. If their actions exhibit goodness, kindness, gentleness, self-control, and so on, then we feel confident in saying that person is good.

Of course, we know that no one is good in and of himself. Without receiving the work of Jesus on the cross, there is nothing good in any of us. But with His spirit residing inside you? Girl, you can be really, really good.

I get it, Lord. It's Your goodness, not my own. Your work on the cross made me good. I want people to say, "Wow, she's a good person." But I pray that my actions always lead them straight back to You! Amen.

HIS GOODNESS PASSES BEFORE YOU

*And he said, "I will make all my goodness pass before
you and will proclaim before you my name 'The LORD.'
And I will be gracious to whom I will be gracious,
and will show mercy on whom I will show mercy."*

EXODUS 33:19 ESV

Today's verse is fascinating, isn't it? God told Moses that He would make His goodness pass before him. He went on to say that He would be gracious to whom He would be gracious and would show mercy on whom He would show mercy. We have an indicator here that God is deliberate in how and where He shows favor.

Maybe you have sensed God's presence. Perhaps you have witnessed His goodness passing before you and had no doubt it was the very hand of God pouring it out. Consider yourself blessed! Recognize His favor! He's going above and beyond in moments like that.

If only the world could see the goodness of God the way you do. Oh, but they can! When you live for Him, when you share His heart with others, His goodness becomes apparent to all. You become a beacon of hope to a lost world when you live like this.

*Thank You for blessing me so abundantly, Lord! May
I be unstoppable in sharing Your goodness with those
around me so that they might know You. Amen.*

HIS STEADFAST LOVE

Oh give thanks to the LORD, for he is good,
for his steadfast love endures forever!

PSALM 107:1 ESV

God's love is steadfast. It's never ending, never changing, never fluctuating. He doesn't love you less today than He did yesterday, nor does He love you more. He couldn't possibly love you any more than He already does.

That's crazy to think about, isn't it? We human beings tend to love in increments, depending on how we are treated. We often repay evil for evil and good for good.

But God isn't like that. His steadfast love is unstoppable. Even if you mess up in a royal way, His goodness toward you won't change one iota. (Hint: this isn't an invitation to misbehave! He's hoping you'll line up and walk straight!)

How remarkable to realize that God is undeterred by our flaws! If only we could live like that and treat others with such goodness in our hearts.

Jesus, I want to follow Your example! I want to learn to be steadfast
in my love for others and in my goodness toward them. May my
affections never be conditional. Show me how to love like You. Amen.

OVERCOME EVIL WITH GOOD

Do not be overcome by evil, but overcome evil with good.

ROMANS 12:21 ESV

Turn on the evening news and you are sure to be overwhelmed with the goings-on being reported. World chaos. Health crises. Political upheaval. Divisions. Media control. It's difficult to know who to believe or who to trust. And in these uncertain times, it's easy to add to the division already happening on social media. Sometimes you just feel driven to get your point across. You can't seem to help yourself.

Of course, God has a better plan. When you're surrounded by evil, He wants to remind you that you can overcome that evil with good.

Don't allow yourself to be drawn in, girl! Don't get pulled down the rabbit hole. Stay focused on Him. Keep your hope and your faith intact. And then do your best to lift the hearts and the spirits of others along the way.

Lord, I don't want to get sucked into the chaos. There's so much evil swirling around me at times that I feel overwhelmed. Thank You for the reminder that I can truly overcome evil with Your unstoppable goodness. Good outweighs bad any day! Amen.

UNSTOPPABLE FAITHFULNESS

"One who is faithful in a very little is also faithful in much, and one who is dishonest in a very little is also dishonest in much. If then you have not been faithful in the unrighteous wealth, who will entrust to you the true riches? And if you have not been faithful in that which is another's, who will give you that which is your own?"

LUKE 16:10–12 ESV

He who is faithful in little is faithful in much.

Maybe you've witnessed this in your own life. Perhaps when you were a young adult you struggled to handle your finances properly. You didn't make much money at the time, but neither did you spend it the way you should have. Now you are older and wiser. You have learned from your mistakes. You are now faithful with your finances, and God is giving you opportunities to earn more than ever.

His increase in provision is a visible demonstration of His faithfulness. He's giving you a second chance, an opportunity to do better this time around. See how diligent He is? See how forgiving?

God is unstoppable when it comes to His faithfulness in your life. He won't let you down. He has you covered, fully and completely.

I know I can trust You, Lord. You've proved Yourself faithful time and time again in my life. How I love You, my unstoppable God. Amen.

BIND THEM AROUND YOUR NECK

Let not steadfast love and faithfulness forsake you; bind them around your neck; write them on the tablet of your heart. So you will find favor and good success in the sight of God and man.

PROVERBS 3:3–4 ESV

God's faithfulness is tried and true. He's incapable of being unfaithful to you. That's what kind of unstoppable heavenly Father you have—the kind who never gives up on you.

He longs for you to have that same kind of faithfulness to Him. He doesn't want you to be a flighty lover, always looking in different directions for the next great thing or something else to satisfy your soul. No, He longs for your whole heart. He's a jealous lover, One who wants to keep you to Himself.

God wants you to write the word *faithful* on the tablet of your heart, to bind it like a necklace around your neck so that you never forget that you are His and He is yours.

Today, commit to walk faithfully with Him, no matter how difficult life might get.

Jesus, I am binding my faithfulness to You like a necklace. I'm keeping You close to my heart. I won't walk away. I won't abandon this beautiful relationship with my unstoppable God. Amen.

HE CAN'T DENY HIMSELF

If we are faithless, he remains faithful—for he cannot deny himself.
2 TIMOTHY 2:13 ESV

When you spoke the words, you really meant them. You pledged your faithfulness—to that friend, that spouse, that child. But then you broke their trust. You did the opposite of what you intended. And in the process, you broke a heart.

Aren't you glad God isn't like that? If He says He will remain faithful to you, He will! You don't have to wonder if He's going to slip up and make a mistake or gossip about you behind your back. His faithfulness is solid. Rock solid.

And God longs for you to learn from His example. No matter how many people you've hurt, no matter how many mistakes you've made, it's not too late to take on the attributes of Christ and become more faithful to those you love and to Him.

Jesus, I want to be more like You! I don't want to hurt others. I don't want to break any more hearts. And I don't want to break Your heart either. May I become like You, my unstoppable, faithful God. Amen.

HE COVERS YOU WITH HIS FEATHERS

*He will cover you with his feathers, and under his wings you will
find refuge; his faithfulness will be your shield and rampart.*

PSALM 91:4 NIV

Today's verse offers a beautiful illustration of God's faithfulness to
you, His child! He covers you with His feathers. He is your Refuge,
your Safe Place. Doesn't that image bring joy to your heart?

The bird's wing is both strong and gentle. Like a mama hen
guarding her baby chicks under her wing, you are safely tucked away
under the holy care of your unstoppable God.

Think about this for a moment: His wing isn't weighty. It will
not crush you. It won't add to your already burdened heart. Instead, it
will spread wide to encompass you when you're going through a hard
time and will actually ease your burden. Tucked away under His wing,
you'll realize just how much He cares. You'll find solutions. You'll feel
His heartbeat and be assured of His vast love for you.

What a loving, gracious, faithful, unstoppable God we serve! Oh,
to spend more time with Him!

*I'm so grateful for Your wings of protection, Father! Thank You for
covering me with Your feathers and for loving me so beautifully. Amen.*

A WAY OF ESCAPE

*No temptation has overtaken you that is not common to man.
God is faithful, and he will not let you be tempted beyond
your ability, but with the temptation he will also provide
the way of escape, that you may be able to endure it.*

1 CORINTHIANS 10:13 ESV

Have you ever visited a corn maze? They're a lot of fun, but they can be tricky to navigate. Just when you think you've found an escape route, you're trapped in another corner. You twist, you turn, but you're still lost. It takes a while to finally weasel your way out.

Sometimes life is like a corn maze. You're sure about a decision, and so you turn to the right only to realize you've hit a dead end. Then you turn around and begin again, only to get lost once more. Ugh! What a mess!

Aren't you glad walking with God isn't like that? He always provides a way of escape, even if you are in a maze of your own making. No matter how far you've fallen, no matter how deep the sin, you can turn to Him and He will point you toward the exit so that you can enjoy freedom—totally, fully, eternally. What a marvelous, faithful God to provide a way of escape!

*Thank You for providing a way out for me, Lord! I've gotten myself
into some real jams over the years, but You always provide a way
of escape, even when I don't deserve it. How I praise You. Amen.*

THE CROWN OF LIFE

"Do not fear what you are about to suffer. Behold, the devil is about to throw some of you into prison, that you may be tested, and for ten days you will have tribulation. Be faithful unto death, and I will give you the crown of life."

REVELATION 2:10 ESV

We don't like to think about suffering. In fact, we hope to avoid the topic altogether. But we live in a broken world. Pain exists. Chaos exists. And humanity is careening toward the fulfillment of end-times prophecies at what feels like warp speed.

God wants you to remain steadfast and faithful, even when everything around you is swirling or feeling strangely unfamiliar. You can still be consistent. Yes, you will have problems. Yes, you will experience tribulations and even pain. But you were born for this. With the power of the Spirit, you can see this thing through. He'll go with you every step of the way. Even if there's suffering involved, you can come through this journey closer to God and stronger in your faith.

God has been faithful. And now, when the world is shaking, He wants to convince you that you can be faithful as well.

I get it, Lord. I can be faithful even during the shaking. Help me, I pray! Amen.

NO FALSE FAITHFULNESS

But I will not take my love from him,
nor will I ever betray my faithfulness.

PSALM 89:33 NIV

You know the type. She claims to be your BFF, your bestie, and then when your back is turned she gossips about you or spreads lies. You've learned the hard way who can be trusted and who cannot. To your face there's always a bright smile and the pretense of friendship, but behind your back? That's another thing altogether.

Aren't you glad that God doesn't operate like that? His faithfulness is true. It's honest. There are no fake smiles from Him. That grin on His face? It's the real deal, and it's there because He adores you, His precious child.

Your faithful God will never let you down. Others will, sure. And no doubt you will let a few of them down as well. But when it comes to your relationship with your unstoppable God? You can trust Him from start to finish.

There's nothing fake or false about You, Jesus. I'm so grateful
You are trustworthy. I'm so grateful You won't hurt me when
my back is turned. May I be just as faithful to You. Amen.

ABOUNDING IN STEADFAST LOVE AND FAITHFULNESS

The LORD passed before him and proclaimed, "The LORD, the LORD, a God merciful and gracious, slow to anger, and abounding in steadfast love and faithfulness."

EXODUS 34:6 ESV

How much does God love you? Have you ever wondered? Just how deep is His faithfulness toward you? Some people get hung up on this. They think God's love must be conditional in the same way human love is. Fortunately, that's not true! His love is limitless.

The Bible says that your unstoppable God abounds in steadfast love and faithfulness. To abound in something means you always have more. And more. And more. It's a never-ending flow, like water coming over a waterfall. With that in mind, God must love you infinitely!

Today's verse also reminds us that God's love is steadfast. It's consistent. Persistent. It never gives up. Even when we try to run in the opposite direction, He keeps pouring it out. It's not contingent upon our behavior. Thank goodness, right? (Otherwise we'd be in a world of trouble!)

What a wonderful, steadfast, faithful God we serve!

Thank You, Lord, for pouring out Your love and faithfulness even when I don't deserve it. You always have more for me. I bask in the never-ending flow, my unstoppable God! Amen.

I WON'T CONCEAL IT

I have not hidden your deliverance within my heart; I have spoken of your faithfulness and your salvation; I have not concealed your steadfast love and your faithfulness from the great congregation. As for you, O Lord, you will not restrain your mercy from me; your steadfast love and your faithfulness will ever preserve me!

PSALM 40:10–11 ESV

These days it's not easy to talk about God openly. The Gospel message flies in the face of our modern, so-called progressive culture. Folks seem to be progressing away from Him, sadly, and many of them expect us to do the same. (They're not fans of our belief system, to be sure!)

But God wants us to speak up! He's been faithful to us, so why would we not be faithful to tell others about Him? Shout the Gospel message from the rooftops so all can hear!

Don't conceal your relationship with Jesus from the masses. Don't hide away in a corner, hoping others won't notice you. He wants you to shine like a city on a hill, always ready to tell others what He has done in your life.

Speak up, sister! Your unstoppable God is counting on it.

Give me courage, I pray, Lord. I want to speak up more and more in these troubling times. May I never be afraid of what others will think. May I speak boldly of Your steadfast love and faithfulness to all I meet. Amen.

NO WAVERING

*Let us hold unswervingly to the hope we
profess, for he who promised is faithful.*

HEBREWS 10:23 NIV

If you've ever been out on a rowboat in rough waters, you know what
the word *wavering* means. If you attempted to stand up in the boat,
it could tip over!

God doesn't want your faith to waver. He wants you to be as
sturdy as an oak tree, as solid as a rock. He longs for you to hold fast
to the confession of your hope without teetering to the right or the
left with every changing wind, whether it's political, health related,
or otherwise. Why? Because He has been faithful to you. You owe
Him complete faithfulness in return.

Take a deep breath, sister. You can do this without toppling
overboard if you keep your focus on God.

*You've been faithful to me, my unstoppable God! How could I ever
betray You or get caught up in the current of confusion that this world
is throwing my way? May I be as sturdy as an oak tree, I pray. Amen.*

UNSTOPPABLE GENTLENESS

*But in your hearts honor Christ the Lord as holy, always being
prepared to make a defense to anyone who asks you for a reason
for the hope that is in you; yet do it with gentleness and respect.*

1 PETER 3:15 ESV

When you read, "Do it with gentleness and respect," what comes to
mind? It's not always easy to handle tough relationships with gentleness and respect, is it? And yet if you pause to think about how
gentle, how sweet God has been to you over the years, you begin to
see that this has been His plan all along.

Your unstoppable heavenly Father could have chosen to treat you
harshly, but instead—out of His abundant love for you—He chose
grace. Mercy, gentleness.

And now He's asking the same from you. Can you operate in
unstoppable gentleness toward others? Even in the heat of the battle?
When things are going wrong at work? When the kids are disobey-
ing? It might seem impossible, but with God all things are possible.
Unstoppable gentleness, girl. It's the Father's heart for you.

*Thank You for Your gentleness with me over the years,
Lord. I'm so grateful. I want to learn from You so
that I can be gentle with others as well. Amen.*

A SOFT ANSWER

A gentle answer turns away anger, but a sharp word causes anger.
PROVERBS 15:1 NLV

When was the last time you offered someone a soft answer? Maybe you got riled up at your boss and wanted to tell him off after he humiliated you in front of your coworkers—but you didn't. Or perhaps you had a disagreement with your spouse over finances and things got testy. Everything inside you wanted to blow up—but you chose not to.

It really is possible to offer a soft answer, even when someone comes at you with harsh words. Yes, it often requires a deep breath first. Perhaps a silent prayer, ushered heavenward for God's intervention. But think of it this way: How many times has He responded with a soft answer to you instead of a harsh word?

People are more likely to respond to gentleness than to bitterness or anger. So, do your best to remain gentle with all. In exchange, they will treat you with the kindness and gentleness you deserve, girl. That's a win-win!

Your soft answers have molded and shaped my life, Lord! I'm so grateful for the many times when You could have been harsh with me but chose gentleness instead. I want to be more like You in this way. Amen.

SPEAK EVIL OF NO ONE

*Remind them. . .to speak evil of no one, to avoid quarreling,
to be gentle, and to show perfect courtesy toward all people.*

TITUS 3:1–2 ESV

Take a close look at today's passage. *Speak evil of no one. Avoid quarreling. Be gentle. Show perfect courtesy toward all people.*

Yikes! Perhaps you didn't know these verses were even in the Bible! Jesus longs for us to speak kindly of others? Doesn't He see how mean they are to us? According to this passage, He doesn't want us to speak ill of anyone, even in the midst of a battle!

How difficult is that? When someone is clearly wrong and they are coming at you like a bull in a china shop, you probably want to lash out, to tell everyone just how wrong they are. But even then, God's way involves a path of gentleness, not hasty, angry gossip.

So, take a deep breath, girl. This one's going to take some work. Can you lay down your angst long enough to allow God's Spirit to intervene in your heart? If so, then you will become more and more like your unstoppable, gentle heavenly Father.

*I have to admit, this is a tough one, Lord! When I'm under
attack, I just want to lash out, to make my voice heard. But You're
teaching me that You have a better way. May I learn to walk in
the way of gentleness so that I can be more like You. Amen.*

SUPPORTED BY HIS RIGHT HAND

*You have given me your shield of victory. Your right
hand supports me; your help has made me great.*

PSALM 18:35 NLT

Imagine you're walking with a friend down the sidewalk when suddenly you trip over a crack and take off flying! Your friend reaches out a gentle hand and takes you by the arm. Suddenly you are steady on your feet once more. Your friend didn't have to say a word. His presence, his quick actions, kept you from tumbling.

God is that friend with the gentle right hand. He sees the cracks in the sidewalk even before you do. He's keenly aware of the temptations in front of you, the ones that could cause you to fall and make a spectacle of yourself. But He's right there, ready to guard and protect. Ready to stand in the gap. Without saying a word, He will support you with His gentleness and love. What a precious, wonderful Friend He is!

*You care so deeply for me, my unstoppable God!
I'm grateful for Your gentle right hand, which holds
me up and supports me, keeping me from danger. Amen.*

THEY MAY COME TO THEIR SENSES

*And the Lord's servant must not be quarrelsome but kind to everyone,
able to teach, patiently enduring evil, correcting his opponents with
gentleness. God may perhaps grant them repentance leading to a
knowledge of the truth, and they may come to their senses and escape
from the snare of the devil, after being captured by him to do his will.*

2 TIMOTHY 2:24–26 ESV

Why do you suppose God wants you to be patient and gentle, even
with your opponents? Could it be that some of them might discover
the error of their ways if you take the time to coach them through
the issue? Could they really come to their senses and, as today's Bible
reading says, escape the snare of the devil?

Perhaps if we took the time to respond gently and kindly, even
in the heat of the battle, we might see for ourselves that God is supernatural and can touch the hearts of even the hardest people. He's
in the business of turning lives around, after all!

So who came to mind immediately when you read the words
hardest people? Did a face flash before your eyes? Perhaps this is the
very person you need to pray for today! Your gentle, loving heavenly
Father wants nothing more than to see that person come to know
Him, and you can play a role by simply treating that person with the
gentleness of your unstoppable God.

*I get it, Jesus. My gentleness toward others can have a positive outcome.
They might come to know You, to discover a whole new way of living, as
I have. Guard my tongue, I pray. May I be as gentle as a lamb. Amen.*

CHECK YOUR MOTIVES!

*But the wisdom that comes from heaven is first of
all pure; then peace-loving, considerate, submissive,
full of mercy and good fruit, impartial and sincere.*

JAMES 3:17 NIV

Today's verse requires a bit of unpacking. It contains a lot of information in just a few words. God's wisdom is first pure. Let's stop right there. If you examined the motives of your heart, especially during an argument with a friend, say, would your motives always be pure and holy? Probably not.

If you make sure your motives are good, then everything else that follows in this verse will come into alignment. Good motives lead to peace, gentleness, a voice of reason. Good motives are filled with good fruit and mercy for others. Good motives mean that you will be impartial and sincere, even when dealing with those who are tough cases.

Check your motives, sister! It could be the problem starts right there.

*Ouch! This is a tough one, Lord! You've called me to be gentle, peaceable,
open to reason. But sometimes I can't see past my own stubbornness
and pride to get there. Check my motives. Examine my heart. Make
me more like You, my unstoppable, gentle heavenly Father. Amen.*

RESTORE HIM IN A
SPIRIT OF GENTLENESS

*Brothers, if anyone is caught in any transgression, you who
are spiritual should restore him in a spirit of gentleness.
Keep watch on yourself, lest you too be tempted.*

GALATIANS 6:1 ESV

Usually when someone messes up, especially if their transgression
affects us personally, we want to give him or her a piece of our mind.
We're more than happy to bring correction but rarely in a grace-filled,
gentle way. Oh no! We're ready to blast them, to let them have it!

Today's verse encourages us to bring our corrections in a spirit of
gentleness. Ouch. That's not always easy, is it? In fact, you might be
wondering if such a thing is even possible! It is, but doing so requires
moving your pride aside and caring more about that person and the
outcome than you do about your feelings.

Sure, you want to get your point across, but at what cost? Are you
willing to lose a friend or perhaps turn someone away from God? No,
it's always better to bring correction in love. That is your unstoppable
God's way.

*I want to be more like You in this way, Jesus!
May I be gentle in all I say and do. Amen.*

TAKE HIS YOKE UPON YOU

*"Take my yoke upon you, and learn from me, for I am gentle
and lowly in heart, and you will find rest for your souls."*

MATTHEW 11:29 ESV

Jesus commands us to "take His yoke" upon ourselves. But what
does this mean? In biblical times a yoke was hand-carved to fit the
shoulders of the animals. It was made in such a way that it yoked
the animals together without causing any pain. In short, the animal
submitted itself to the yoking process, knowing it would be well
taken care of.

Isn't that a fascinating image? Jesus is asking you to link yourself
to Him. And He is assuring you in this verse that His yoke is easy.
It's not meant to cause pain. It's simply a way of binding yourself to
Him so that He can carry the brunt of the load.

Face it. . .you're getting a little tired hauling that load around
anyway. So hands off. Let Him take it. Once you finally let go, you're
going to feel really, really good.

*Thank You for Your easy yoke, Jesus! I'm happy to submit to Your
authority in my life, knowing that You will protect me. And thank
You for carrying the load! Whew! What a relief, Lord! Amen.*

WOOED BY GENTLENESS

Be completely humble and gentle; be patient,
bearing with one another in love.

EPHESIANS 4:2 NIV

We are drawn to gentle people. Think about how easy it is to come into the presence of God, knowing that you can bring Him any of your transgressions without fear of retribution or anger. His gentleness woos you. It makes you feel safe and secure. You don't fear an angry response. Never!

The people God has placed in your life need that same assurance from you. They will be comfortable opening up and sharing their sorrows only if they feel you are gentle and trustworthy. Sure, you might have to speak hard truth in love should the situation call for it. But don't assume that. Just be willing. Available.

Make sharing easy for them. Offer a cup of coffee, a cozy spot to settle down for a chat, and a warm, open heart filled with gentleness, no matter what they might confess. Your friend will gain a confidant for life, and you will be leading in the way your heavenly Father would want you to lead. That's a win for everyone involved!

I want to have an open-door policy, Lord! May others come to me
knowing they will have the assurance of a gentle response from a kind
and loving heart. Make me more like You, my unstoppable God. Amen.

LIKE A SHEPHERD

*He will tend his flock like a shepherd; he will gather
the lambs in his arms; he will carry them in his
bosom, and gently lead those that are with young.*

ISAIAH 40:11 ESV

Have you ever thought about the temperament of a shepherd? Most
are referenced as being kind and patient. Let's face it—a cruel shepherd
wouldn't hold on to his sheep for very long, would he? Those little
babes would escape every chance they got with a mean shepherd over
them! They would run for the gate every time it opened. But sheep
respond well to a loving shepherd, one who leads with patience and
gentle firmness.

God wants you to be a gentle shepherd—in how you love your
children, in how you love others, in how you speak to strangers. You
can gather them like lambs in your arms if you approach them gently,
sweetly. Oh, it's not always easy. You might want to pop off, to let
your temper flare. But God has a better plan. You can do it, girl. You
can go easy on people, loving them the way Christ does. This is how
a true leader leads, like a gentle shepherd.

*I'll admit it, Lord—I don't always go easy on people. I'm not
always gentle. Sometimes I really lose my cool! But I want to
follow Your lead, my gentle Shepherd. Help me, I pray. Amen.*

UNSTOPPABLE SELF-CONTROL

*A man without self-control is like a city
broken into and left without walls.*

PROVERBS 25:28 ESV

Your unstoppable God wants you to have unstoppable self-control. Ouch! This is a tough one! To have self-control means you have the ability to stop yourself midstream to prevent a catastrophe from happening! Right when those ugly words are about to escape your lips. Just as you're about to slam down the phone and end the conversation. (Ever been there?)

Right then, in the heat of the battle, you can exhibit self-control. How? By following the lead of Jesus Christ, the epitome of self-control. He thought of others first when He went to the cross. He had you on His mind when He died and rose again. He wasn't hyperfocused on "me, myself, and I" like folks in modern-day culture. No, Jesus always thought of others. And because they were in the forefront of His mind, self-control came naturally. (Hint: it's easier to control yourself when you're not in it to prove you're always right.)

You can do this, girl. Take a breath. Count to ten. You've got this.

*Lord, I get it! You want me to have the same self-control
You exhibited. It won't be easy, but with You on my side,
I know anything (even this!) is possible. Amen.*

HE GAVE IT AS A GIFT

The Spirit God gave us does not make us timid,
but gives us power, love and self-discipline.

2 TIMOTHY 1:7 NIV

"I don't have any self-control," you say as you reach for the tub of ice cream. "I just can't do it!" you moan as you give in to that same old sin one more time.

And yet you were created in the image of a perfect, unstoppable God, One who has all the self-control you could ever imagine! His Word is filled with passages—like the one above—meant to convince you! So, bye-bye, excuses. Hello, possibilities!

With God on your side, you can do it. You *can* say no to temptation. You *can* turn away from situations that draw you in. You *can* bite your tongue instead of lashing out.

Self-control is a gift, straight from your heavenly Father. He poured it out, knowing it would bring power with it. Power for what, you ask? Power to say, "I don't think so!" when someone tempts you to do or say the wrong thing. Power to make a better choice. Power to live a different sort of life than you have lived in the past.

Embrace this gift today. Celebrate it, and experience new life, new outcomes!

Lord, I'm so grateful for the gift of self-control! Oh, how I need it!
Rid me of excuses, I pray. I turn away from them even now and
embrace the power that comes with this remarkable gift. Amen.

THE PERFECT SUPPLEMENT

*For this very reason, make every effort to supplement your faith with
virtue, and virtue with knowledge, and knowledge with self-control,
and self-control with steadfastness, and steadfastness with godliness,
and godliness with brotherly affection, and brotherly affection with love.*

2 PETER 1:5–7 ESV

Supplements have become very popular in recent years. The more we
learn about how our food is produced, the more we realize our need
for supplemental vitamins and minerals.

God has a supplement that He recommends as well. Today's
scripture clues us in. He wants us to make every effort to supplement
our faith with virtue and to supplement our virtue with knowledge.
The list goes on from there, but midway down we find the word
self-control. This is one of many supplements that God hopes you will
add to your daily regimen.

He doesn't *just* want you to have self-control but to be steadfast
in the way you approach it. Be diligent. Consistent. Don't be like that
dieter who is on again off again, behaving one day but misbehaving
the next. No, when it comes to your faith walk, let self-control be the
rule of law. Your heavenly Father knows that you will be unstoppable
once you learn to live like this.

*Thank You for giving me these amazing supplements, Lord.
I want to be as strong as I can be in You. Help me, I pray. Amen.*

RULE YOUR SPIRIT

*Better to be patient than powerful; better to
have self-control than to conquer a city.*

PROVERBS 16:32 NLT

Everyone wants to be seen as tough. Mighty. We humans don't like
to appear vulnerable, especially to our enemies! (There's nothing
worse, right?)

Interestingly, God has a different plan! His prescription for success
can be found in today's verse. He commands us to rule our spirits. We
are to exhibit self-control in the way we respond to others. Instead of
lashing out in anger (which some "mighty" people do), we are better
served to stay calm, cool, and collected. When we take the time to
rule our spirits, we come out winners in the end.

So, what areas of your life do you need to bring under kingdom
rule? What areas are out of control? Look at them honestly. With a
careful eye. Then ask the Lord to help you craft a plan to tackle those
weak areas. Before long, you will be strong and mighty, completely
ruled by His Spirit!

*Thank You for the reminder, my unstoppable God, that I
can get all areas of my life under control, even the ones that
have eluded me. Rule my spirit, I pray, Lord! Amen.*

THE ATHLETE YOU
WERE CALLED TO BE

Do you not know that in a race all the runners run, but only one receives the prize? So run that you may obtain it. Every athlete exercises self-control in all things. They do it to receive a perishable wreath, but we an imperishable. So I do not run aimlessly; I do not box as one beating the air. But I discipline my body and keep it under control, lest after preaching to others I myself should be disqualified.

1 CORINTHIANS 9:24–27 ESV

Perhaps you read the title of today's devotion and laughed. Maybe you consider yourself to be anything but an athlete. Here's a fun truth: your unstoppable God wants you to be unstoppable in the way you run your race. There are many runners, after all, but only one receives the prize.

This passage from 1 Corinthians brings up a clear point, that every athlete is to exercise self-control in all things. Stop to think about that for a moment. How does she exhibit self-control? In her diligence to keep running, sure. But it starts before that, actually. She is diligent in her lifestyle choices. Diet, exercise, daily routine. Stretching the muscles, running, even when she doesn't feel like it.

Self-control certainly plays a big role in running the race, sister. So what's keeping you from the starting block? Ready, set, run!

Thank You for the reminder that I can win this race as long as I exercise self-control along the way. I will keep going, Lord! I will be unstoppable. Amen.

DISCIPLINE YOUR BODY

But I discipline my body and keep it under control, lest after preaching to others I myself should be disqualified.

1 CORINTHIANS 9:27 ESV

Let's face it—we don't always feel like disciplining our bodies. Exercising, watching what we eat, staying away from harmful, addictive traits—these things aren't easy to do! It's so much easier to order a pizza and lounge around on the sofa than to eat a healthy meal and work out. (Can I get a witness?)

Here's one problem with taking the easy road: our unstoppable God wants us to take the harder way. (Ouch!) The disciplined way. The self-controlled way. The "I'd better get up off this sofa and get to work" way.

Our heavenly Father knows that we will truly be unstoppable only if we are in good health. Getting there requires work on our part. So get up off that sofa, girl. Drop that ice cream cone. Do the hard things. And in the end, you will be healthier for it.

Thank You for the reminder that I need to be self-controlled when it comes to my diet and exercise, Lord. This might not be easy, but I'm willing to give it a try. Help me, I pray! Amen.

FOR THE SAKE OF YOUR PRAYERS

*The end of all things is at hand; therefore be self-controlled
and sober-minded for the sake of your prayers.*

1 PETER 4:7 ESV

Today's verse is an interesting one, isn't it? God admonishes us to
be self-controlled, but look at His reasoning—"for the sake of your
prayers." Hold on a minute, Lord! Are you saying that the outcome
of my prayers is dependent on my own personal self-control, or is
there something more to this?

Think about it this way: Imagine you're off on a tangent, living
away from God. Far away. You're doing your own thing, dabbling in
all sorts of mischief. Suddenly a crisis occurs. You have a sudden desire
to bring an urgent prayer request to God. But since you've been so
far removed from Him, you're overwhelmed with guilt. Will He still
welcome you? Will He still care about the things you care about?

If you want to do away with those feelings of shame as you approach His throne, then live a self-controlled life. Lay down your selfish
desires and follow after Him. Then—if and when crises occur—you
can approach boldly, unashamed.

*Lord, I let myself fall so far at times. I always live to regret it.
You welcome me back so lovingly and graciously, but I can't help
but feel shame. Show me how to live with self-control leading the
way so that I can lay down my shame once and for all! Amen.*

A LOVER OF GOOD

An overseer. . .must be. . .hospitable, a lover of good,
self-controlled, upright, holy, and disciplined.

TITUS 1:7–8 ESV

There are two ways to look at self-control: one is to view it as a rule, a law from God. The other is to fall in love with the notion of doing good and wanting to please God as a result of your love.

Can you see the difference? Rules versus grace. Rules versus love and passion. One is restrictive and makes you feel closed in. The other offers total and complete freedom, along with a burst of heavenly peace. You can change how you view self-control today. You can begin to see it as an avenue to freedom.

Your unstoppable God wants you to be a lover of good. It's not enough to follow the rules. It's not enough to behave for the sake of behaving. There are areas of your life that need to come under control, not because God is trying to whip you into shape, but because He wants your heart. Give them to Him today, and then watch as He grows you into a woman of great self-control.

I get it, Lord! You are after my heart. You're not trying to turn me
into a rule follower. You long to be in relationship with me. Amen.

IN THIS PRESENT AGE

For the grace of God has been revealed, bringing salvation to all people. And we are instructed to turn from godless living and sinful pleasures. We should live in this evil world with wisdom, righteousness, and devotion to God, while we look forward with hope to that wonderful day when the glory of our great God and Savior, Jesus Christ, will be revealed. He gave his life to free us from every kind of sin, to cleanse us, and to make us his very own people, totally committed to doing good deeds.

TITUS 2:11–14 NLT

Sometimes we say things like this: "But you don't understand! It's so hard to be a person of faith today. The world opposes us at every turn!"

That's true, but remember—there's nothing new under the sun. Believers have always faced opposing forces. They've always had foes. Persecution has always taken place. Life for the believer has rarely been easy.

Sure, it feels like opposition to people of faith is ramping up in recent years, but think about the early church—believers in the first century, for example. What a struggle they faced! And yet somehow they lived self-controlled, upright, godly lives in their "present age," just as we are admonished to do today.

God wants you to remain strong, sister! Hang in there, no matter how tough things get. Be brave. Be upright. And hold on to your self-control. It's going to be more important than ever.

*Lord, I am grateful for the reminder that my journey—
hard as it might be—is doable! I won't give up, no
matter how many opposing forces I face. Amen.*

AN IMPERISHABLE PRIZE

*Every athlete exercises self-control in all things. They do it
to receive a perishable wreath, but we an imperishable.*

1 CORINTHIANS 9:25 ESV

Athletes enter races to win prizes. Trophies. Medals. Media attention.
All these things are theirs for the taking if they come in first place. Of
course, the gal who comes in ninth doesn't go home with a physical
reminder of her achievement. She does, however, have the satisfaction
of knowing she completed her race.

We're after a different sort of prize, aren't we? Yes, God has called
us to run a race, to be diligent and self-controlled. But our ultimate goal
isn't to bring home a medal. We are longing for home—for heaven.
Our prize isn't perishable. It won't dissolve into dust after we're gone
from this earth. When we "win" Jesus, we win eternity. We get forever
with Him. Talk about the ultimate satisfaction!

Now you see the benefit of running a diligent race! When you stay
the course, when you keep your heart, mind, and strength focused on
Him, it's because you're wanting to please the One you plan to spend
eternity with. Now, that's a race worth winning!

*Lord, I'll keep running. I will keep my eyes on You, my ultimate prize.
I won't be distracted by temporal prizes. What I'm after, Jesus, is You!
What a wonderful time we'll have spending eternity together! Amen.*

UNSTOPPABLE WISDOM

If any of you lacks wisdom, let him ask God, who gives
generously to all without reproach, and it will be given him.

JAMES 1:5 ESV

Your unstoppable God longs for you to have unstoppable wisdom. You might read that and ask, "How? How in the world can my wisdom be unstoppable?"

Today's verse offers a terrific clue: ask. It's really that simple. What you lack in wisdom, God can give you in an instant. In fact, He gives generously without reproach. In other words, you don't have to feel guilty for asking. You're not burdening Him with your request. (Whew! You can approach Him boldly!)

Why does God remind you to ask for wisdom? Because it differs so greatly from worldly knowledge. It can't be learned in a book or classroom. There's no diploma or certificate to prove it. Wisdom is absorbed through the Spirit, a gift straight from your heavenly Father.

It's great to gain knowledge, of course. Study hard. Learn all you can. But while you're at it, ask for a double dose of Spirit-driven wisdom! That's what you'll really need to succeed.

Lord, I get it! You want to pour out more. . .and more. . .and more.
So today I ask for more godly wisdom that I might better serve
You. I thank You in advance, my unstoppable God! Amen.

OPEN TO REASON

The wisdom from above is first of all pure. It is also peace loving, gentle at all times, and willing to yield to others. It is full of mercy and the fruit of good deeds. It shows no favoritism and is always sincere.

JAMES 3:17 NLT

When you're open to reason, you don't come into a conversation with an argumentative spirit. Yes, you might think you're right, but you're open to the notion that you might not be. (That's true wisdom right there—acknowledging that you're not always right!)

Your unstoppable God wants to open your heart to the possibility that you still have a few life lessons to learn. When you come into that knowledge with gentleness and a heart open to reason, when you treat others in a sincere way, you can glean understanding from them. And isn't that really a win-win for both of you?

Those rough encounters you've had with friends and loved ones? They can be a thing of the past if you'll simply acknowledge that you're not always right. When you humble yourself and develop a teachable spirit, those know-it-all days will be behind you.

Take a deep breath, girl! You're still on a learning curve—and that's okay.

I don't want to be a know-it-all, Lord! Help me lay down my pride. I still have so many life lessons to learn. May they come easily, I pray! Amen.

MORE PRECIOUS THAN JEWELS

Blessed is the one who finds wisdom, and the one who gets understanding, for the gain from her is better than gain from silver and her profit better than gold. She is more precious than jewels, and nothing you desire can compare with her.

PROVERBS 3:13–15 ESV

Finding wisdom is a bit like playing hide-and-seek. You have to search for it. You certainly won't find it in any of the world's systems. In fact, the world has little to offer but foolishness. Look around you for more than a few seconds and this will become clear! Check out the way people speak to one another and you'll be convinced!

When you take the time to search out true wisdom, however, you find something worth ten thousand times more than you ever dared to dream. It's more precious than any jewels you could ever own.

A woman who gains understanding, a woman who finds wisdom, profits more than someone stumbling upon a treasure chest. Nothing can compare with the jewels of wisdom—not money, not fame, not a university degree. Wisdom is a heavenly gift. And it's yours for the taking! God offers it to you, wrapped in ribbons and bows.

I want to be wise, Lord! Pour out that gift that I might become as precious as a jewel when understanding comes. Amen.

FOOLS DESPISE WISDOM

The fear of the LORD is the beginning of knowledge;
fools despise wisdom and instruction.

PROVERBS 1:7 ESV

Have you ever met a person who refused teaching or training? Hey, they say you can't teach an old dog new tricks, and many of the people you've met over the years have proved that to be true. There are a lot of stubborn folks out there who simply refuse to admit that they are ever wrong. Their minds are made up.

Maybe you've been there a time or two yourself. You've squared your shoulders and double-dog dared anyone to defy you. You made up your mind to prove them wrong if they even tried!

Here's the thing about your unstoppable God. He wants to remind His kids that they are always on a learning curve. Wisdom is something that is gained on an hour-by-hour, minute-by-minute basis as you walk with the Holy Spirit. He teaches. He trains. And He wants you to be pliable in His hands, a ready learner.

Acquire wisdom, sweet woman of God. He will be so glad you did—and so will you!

Jesus, may I be a ready learner! I don't want to be stubborn. I don't want to demand my own way or insist that I'm always right. Soften my heart and remind me that there is still plenty of learning ahead. Amen.

BE CAREFUL HOW YOU WALK

*Be very careful, then, how you live—not as unwise but as wise,
making the most of every opportunity, because the days are evil.
Therefore do not be foolish, but understand what the Lord's will is.*

EPHESIANS 5:15–17 NIV

Sometimes we move blissfully along, completely oblivious to the enemy's plans. He trips us up, and then we wonder how we got caught in his trap. Ugh!

God wants you to walk with your eyes wide open, sister. We are living in dangerous times, and the enemy of your soul is on the prowl, ready to deceive, to wreak havoc, to start trouble in relationships, and to discourage you.

But you don't have to allow any of that to happen! May the eyes of your understanding be enlightened to know his tricks. Don't be fooled by the greatest hypnotist of all! (That devil is a sneaky beast!) Hyperfocus on Jesus and His goodness. Walk as one who is wise, and make the very best use of your time while you are here on planet Earth. The days are evil, but you don't have to fall into the enemy's trap.

*Jesus, I want to be wise! My eyes are wide open. I see what the
enemy is up to on this planet. I see his deceptive practices, his lies, his
deceit, and the turmoil he is causing even now. I come against that
in the name of Jesus, and I stand firm, eyes wide open! Amen.*

IN THE FUTURE

Listen to advice and accept instruction,
that you may gain wisdom in the future.
PROVERBS 19:20 ESV

You've opened yourself up to learning how to do things God's way. Your heart is soft and pliable. You are a willing student, ready to gain all the necessary wisdom for your daily life. Congratulations, girl! Job well done. You've come a long way.

But did you ever consider that you are also gaining wisdom so that you will know how to operate in the future? It's true! The things you're learning today will be helpful for the situations you'll face tomorrow. And the day after that. And the day after that.

This wisdom that you're gleaning from the Holy Spirit will be passed down to your children and their children, a gift that keeps on giving. So don't give up, even when things get hard. Remember, seeds are being planted for future generations. Hang in there, girl, and look with joy toward the days ahead.

Thank You for wisdom that transcends the generations,
Lord! I want to glean as much as I can from Your Spirit,
not just for today but for all my tomorrows. Amen.

RIGHT IN HIS OWN EYES

The way of a fool is right in his own eyes,
but a wise man listens to advice.

PROVERBS 12:15 ESV

You know the type. He's always right. You can't convince him otherwise, even with a litany of facts at your disposal. He refuses to see things any other way but his own. Stubborn, stubborn!

The world is filled with stubborn people. They are stiff. Unwilling to bend. But take a close look at today's verse. The Bible says that the way of a fool is right in his own eyes. No wonder he won't be convinced otherwise! He's blind to truth. A wise man, however? He's willing to listen. He has an open mind, and he is ready to admit that he might not have all the answers.

Where do you stand in all of this? Are you pliable? Or are you always right? Today your unstoppable God wants to remind you that remaining soft and malleable is always best.

Lord, I don't want to be made a fool by my stubbornness. So
many times I am convinced I'm right only to discover later that
I was completely wrong. I would rather be wrong and gain
understanding than to go down a fool! Help me, Jesus. Amen.

FUNNY, NOT FUNNY

*Doing wrong is like a joke to a fool, but wisdom
is pleasure to a man of understanding.*

PROVERBS 10:23 ESV

To a foolish person, "doing wrong" is like a joke. Maybe you've known a few people like this. They deliberately do the wrong thing to get attention. They think they're funny. But you don't share in the laughter, and others don't either. No one sees the humor in flat-out rebellion.

There's nothing funny about deliberate disobedience. It's certainly not funny to God. He's not keen on His kids making a joke out of things that should be serious. And here's the really sad part: no one is laughing in the end. There's coming a day when even the most foolish among us will have to acknowledge the error of their ways.

So keep those eyes open, girl. Your unstoppable God wants you to be wise, not foolish, during these perilous times. Don't be foolish, and stay far away from the ones who choose to behave that way!

*May I never make a joke out of something that is serious to You,
Lord. I don't want to ridicule You or Your ways. May I be found
faithful and ready to acquire Your wisdom, my unstoppable God.*

PSALMS, HYMNS,
AND SPIRITUAL SONGS

*Let the word of Christ dwell in you richly, teaching and
admonishing one another in all wisdom, singing psalms and
hymns and spiritual songs, with thankfulness in your hearts to God.*

COLOSSIANS 3:16 ESV

Here's the really cool thing about walking with your unstoppable God: the more you get to know Him, the closer to Him you are, the more filled with His knowledge you become. Before long, you are like a cup full to overflowing, spilling out on everyone you meet! You're so full of the presence of God that you greet others with psalms, hymns, and spiritual songs. (Hey, there's a song in your heart when you're full of the presence of the Lord!)

Contrast that with the way the world interacts. You see fighting, squabbling, disagreements, and division all around you. People can't wait to tear each other apart. It's like a sport to them, in fact.

But not to you! You have the wisdom of your unstoppable God, and it's making all the difference, not just in your own life but to those around you. So keep a song in your heart, sister! Make merry. Greet your friends with a broad smile on your face. Heaven knows, someone needs to keep the cheer going!

*I want to stick close to You, Jesus! Give me wisdom and
fill me with Your understanding so that my interactions
with others will be holy and pure. Amen.*

AN EAR SEEKING KNOWLEDGE

*The heart of the discerning acquires knowledge, for the
ears of the wise seek it out. A gift opens the way and
ushers the giver into the presence of the great.*

PROVERBS 18:15–16 NIV

What are you seeking? What are you on the lookout for? For some,
the answer would be fame or fortune. Others are looking for that next
romantic relationship or the perfect job. Some are seeking after fancy
houses or expensive clothes.

But you? You have inclined your ear to none of those things.
Instead, you are seeking after Jesus! You want His wisdom. You want
His ways. You desire His heart for others, the kind that puts their
needs first, above your own.

The things of this earth? They hold no appeal to you. Not any-
more. You have tasted and seen that they fail you every time. Your ear
is tilted toward heaven, your eyes ever upward for your soon coming
King. You can't wait, in fact! What a day that will be!

*I'm done with the things of this world, Lord! They don't
bring wisdom. They don't bring understanding. They
certainly don't point me to You. From now on it's You and
me all the way, my unstoppable, wise heavenly Father.*

UNSTOPPABLE MIRACLES

"You stretch out your hand to heal, and signs and wonders are
performed through the name of your holy servant Jesus."

ACTS 4:30 ESV

Some would argue that the days of miracles ended when the last apostle died. They would say, "God doesn't move like that today. He doesn't heal the sick. He doesn't mend relationships. He doesn't take care of financial distresses on your behalf." These naysayers simply refuse to believe that God is still in the miracle-working business.

Oh, but He is! His Word says that He is the same yesterday, today, and forever (Hebrews 13:8). Your miraculous, holy God is unstoppable in His quest to perform the miraculous, not just in your life but in the lives of those you love. If your eyes are open, you might see a few "wonders," even now!

Be on the lookout for everyday miracles. That sick child who is now recovering? That's no coincidence. That unexpected check you received in the mail? Your unstoppable God is hard at work on your behalf. He never changes. Not one little bit. He has plenty of miracles on the horizon for you and those you love.

Thank You, my unchanging, unstoppable God! My eyes are wide
open to the miraculous. I'm so grateful for Your intervention on
my behalf, time and time again. How I praise You. Amen.

FAITH LIKE A MUSTARD SEED

*[Jesus] replied, "Because you have so little faith. Truly
I tell you, if you have faith as small as a mustard seed,
you can say to this mountain, 'Move from here to there,'
and it will move. Nothing will be impossible for you."*

MATTHEW 17:20 NIV

God can take your little and turn it into much. Don't believe it? Offer
Him your broken heart and watch as He transforms it. Offer Him 10
percent of your income and watch Him multiply it to cover every need.
Offer Him your teensy-weensy mustard seed grain of faith and watch
Him supernaturally propel you into a woman of great and remarkable
faith! He doesn't require much from you but is definitely looking for
a willing heart, ready to offer what little you have.

What mustard seed can you give God today? Your unstoppable
heavenly Father will multiply and multiply and multiply again! No,
really! He's going to take what you offer and plant it like a seed in
the ground then sprout it into a tree so large it will shade you for
years to come!

Brace yourself for the miraculous, sister. God has big things for
that willing heart of yours.

*Thank You for multiplying my faith, Lord. You are unstoppable
in the way You change and grow my offerings. They might
seem small, but with You they become magnificent. How
grateful I am for Your multiplication process. Amen.*

118

GREATER WORKS

*"Truly, truly, I say to you, whoever believes in me will
also do the works that I do; and greater works than
these will he do, because I am going to the Father."*

JOHN 14:12 ESV

It's one thing to think of God performing a miracle. It's another thing altogether to imagine Him using *you* to do something miraculous. (Whoa!) And yet, today's verse is a clear indicator that God wants you to be a vessel for the miraculous.

How does that idea settle with you? Can you picture yourself praying for someone and seeing them healed? Do you have the faith to believe that God can truly use you in this day and age? Are you willing to stop everything and pray with someone—in the grocery store, the school hallway, or standing next to the water cooler at work?

He can use you, girl! And He will, if you open yourself up to the possibilities. Oh, the testimonies that will come out of your story if you will begin to believe for the impossible!

*Lord, thank You for reminding me that I am usable! I pray for
miracles to flow as my faith is activated in prayer. Not for my
glory, but for Yours, my unstoppable heavenly Father. Amen.*

119

THE HANDS OF PAUL

God was doing extraordinary miracles by the hands of Paul.
ACTS 19:11 ESV

Some miracles happen from a distance. You pray for a missionary in Afghanistan to be released from his oppressors, and then he is supernaturally set free. (Wow!) Other miracles happen with what the Bible calls laying on of hands. Take a look at today's verse from Acts 19:11 (ESV): "God was doing extraordinary miracles by the hands of Paul."

Miraculous things happened when Paul "laid hands" on those in need. Granted, God doesn't always require a hands-on approach, but we must be willing to activate our faith in situations like these.

Do you have the courage to pray for someone in need? Can you step out of your comfort zone long enough to say to a friend, "Hey, would you mind if we prayed. . .right here, right now?" Rarely will anyone turn down an opportunity to be prayed for, after all! And who knows—God might supernaturally intervene as your hand reaches out to take hold of your friend's.

> *Lord, give me the courage to pray when the situation calls*
> *for it. May I never be intimidated or worried about the*
> *outcome. Activate my faith in the moment, I pray. Amen.*

HE'S MAKING HIS MIGHT KNOWN

*You are the God who performs miracles; you display your
power among the peoples. With your mighty arm you
redeemed your people, the descendants of Jacob and Joseph.*

PSALM 77:14–15 NIV

One way or another, your unstoppable, miraculous God always makes
Himself known to people.

You know it's true, girl! Take a look around you at His remarkable
creation. Those magnificent ocean waves, snowcapped mountaintops,
rushing rivers. They all point to Him! Slithering snakes. Exquisite sea
life. The colors of the rainbow. The shimmer of the moon hovering
overhead. All of nature tells of God's greatness! Don't you get goose
bumps just thinking about the daily displays of His might and power?

Oh, but there's more! A baby's smile. A puppy's tail wagging
back and forth as it cuddles up next to you. The gentle sound of the
cattle lowing in the field. All these things point to your remarkable,
unstoppable Creator. He makes Himself known every moment of
every day, every day of every week, every week of every year. All you
have to do is look around you to see the wonder of who He is. (And
to think, some folks don't believe miracles still take place!)

*I see it, Lord! Your might, Your power, Your wonders—they take my
breath away. How awesome You are, my magnificent Creator. Amen.*

THE HEM OF HIS GARMENT

There was a woman who had had a discharge of blood for twelve years, and though she had spent all her living on physicians, she could not be healed by anyone. She came up behind him and touched the fringe of his garment, and immediately her discharge of blood ceased.

LUKE 8:43–44 ESV

Your unstoppable God has been working miracles from the beginning of time until now. The Bible is filled with stories of people whose lives were impacted because of one moment with the Creator.

Such was the case with the woman with the issue of blood. She had been struggling with a horrible chronic health condition for many, many years. No doctor had been able to help her. But all it took was one touch of the hem of Jesus' garment and she was instantly made whole. Wow! After all that time, just a touch did the trick!

What is it that you need today? What miracle have you been waiting for? Don't give up. No matter how long it takes, keep your faith intact. And then reach out and touch the hem of Jesus' garment. As you do, take that tiny mustard seed of faith and believe, believe, believe!

Lord, I won't give up. I need You so badly. I will stand in faith and believe for a miracle regardless of the circumstances that swirl around me. Amen.

FOR ONE WHO BELIEVES

Jesus asked the boy's father, "How long has he been like this?"
"From childhood," he answered. "It has often thrown him into
fire or water to kill him. But if you can do anything, take pity
on us and help us.""If you can'?" said Jesus. "Everything is
possible for one who believes." Immediately the boy's father
exclaimed, "I do believe; help me overcome my unbelief!"

MARK 9:21–24 NIV

What a story! This boy had been in distress for years. But Jesus told his father that "all things" were possible, if only he could believe.

When you read the words "all things are possible," what comes to mind? Do you immediately doubt, or is your faith activated? Maybe you're thinking of a chronic situation that doesn't seem to be abating, even after much prayer.

In today's scripture, we see a direct correlation between activating our faith and receiving a miracle. All things are possible—for the one who believes.

What are you believing for today? Have you almost given up hope? Have you begun to doubt? Ask the Lord to reactivate your faith, to bring hope to life once more. If you can begin to believe for the impossible, the chances of actually seeing it come to pass are far greater.

You are my unstoppable God, the One who still works
miracles today. Activate my faith, I pray. May I never
give up believing for the impossible. Amen.

HE CONFIRMS THE MESSAGE

They went out and preached everywhere, while the Lord worked with them and confirmed the message by accompanying signs.

MARK 16:20 ESV

Have you ever watched a salesman demonstrate a cleaning product? You would never spend your money on that miracle-working cleanser unless he somehow convinced you that it actually worked.

The same is true when it comes to your faith. God is really good at demonstrating the miraculous so that you can actually believe those messages you read in His Word. He wouldn't tell you that lives could be restored if He didn't actually plan to restore lives. He wouldn't ask you to pray for the sick if He never planned to heal anyone.

Maybe this is why Jesus went around doing so many miracles while He was here on earth. He knew how fickle people can be. They want proof—and He gave it to them, over and over again.

Your unstoppable God is still offering proof, so keep your eyes wide open for the miraculous, sweet sister! It's happening all around you and is meant to activate your faith!

Lord, I get it! You're performing wonders, in part to prove that You can. You're offering a visible demonstration of Your power. My eyes are wide open and my faith is activated, Father!

THEY HUNG AROUND

*So they remained for a long time, speaking boldly for
the Lord, who bore witness to the word of his grace,
granting signs and wonders to be done by their hands.*

ACTS 14:3 ESV

In today's verse, we see an example of a time when the disciples stayed the course. They hung around. They didn't preach a quick Gospel and take off. No, they waited around with the people, speaking boldly all the while. They kept going and going as the Lord did signs and wonders.

Maybe you don't always feel like sticking around. You preach a quick message—possibly chastising someone for something they did wrong—and then hightail it out of there. God wants you to share the truth, sure. But He also wants you to hang around to answer questions. Or pray. Or forgive. Or ask for miracles to follow what you've shared.

Don't be so quick to preach and run, girl! Slow down. People are worth the investment. And who knows? Miracles just might follow if you stick around long enough to watch.

*Lord, I will do my best not to deliver a harsh message and then
bolt and run! I'm in this for the long haul, even in the hardest
of circumstances. Give me courage and strength to see things
through, I pray. People are worth it, after all! Amen.*

IS ANYTHING TOO HARD FOR GOD?

"Behold, I am the LORD, the God of all flesh.
Is anything too hard for me?"
JEREMIAH 32:27 ESV

If someone asked you to make a list of all the things that were too hard for you to accomplish on your own, what would top the list? (The mind reels, right?) No doubt it would be a lengthy list with any number of things you could never possibly do by yourself.

Here's the cool thing about God: nothing is too hard for Him. Literally nothing. If He could spin the world into existence with just a word or two, imagine what He can do in the heart of your loved one. If He could hang the sun in the sky at just the right distance from the earth to warm us and give us light, imagine what He can do in your job situation.

He is capable of the incapable. What we only dream of, He actually does! The impossible becomes possible when you trust Him with it.

So take your hands off, girl. Don't try to handle the situation by yourself. It's beyond you. But it is definitely not beyond your unstoppable God!

Lord, sometimes I forget that You have no limitations! You're a
God of the miraculous! I have shortcomings, but You do not.
So I put my trust in You, my miracle-working Savior! Amen.

UNSTOPPABLE DISCERNMENT

Dear friends, do not believe every spirit, but test the
spirits to see whether they are from God, because
many false prophets have gone out into the world.

1 JOHN 4:1 NIV

Do you ever get it wrong? Like totally and completely wrong?

Example: You think you know someone really well. You trust her. You confide in her. Then you find out she's not at all who she claims to be. She lets you down in a major way. Where was your discernment when you needed it? Surely she left a few clues along the way. How did you miss them?

We don't always get things right, but one thing is for sure: we really can have more discernment if we ask for it. We serve an unstoppable God who gives it to us freely.

Discernment is one gift we desperately need, especially in this day and age! Many people out there claim to be something they're not. Many claim to live for Jesus but don't follow His Word. Don't be pulled in. Test the spirits to see if they are from God.

How is this possible in the moment? When you get that niggling feeling that something is wrong, stop. Pray. Ask God to give you the power to see what's really going on. He will. . .if you ask.

Lord, I need Your unstoppable discernment! I don't want
to get it wrong! I want to trust only the trustworthy ones.
Keep my spiritual eyes and ears open, I pray. Amen.

YOU CAN FIGURE IT OUT

But solid food is for the mature, for those who have their powers of discernment trained by constant practice to distinguish good from evil.

HEBREWS 5:14 ESV

Many people lack discernment. Still others don't care. They don't even try to discern good from bad. They deliberately blur the lines, in fact, hoping no one ever calls them into accountability.

But not you! You want clear lines between right and wrong. Even in this crazy, topsy-turvy world we live in, you desire an honest, above-board walk with the Lord.

Aren't you grateful for the discernment God offers believers? Today's verse assures us that constant practice will increase your powers of discernment. The more you use it, the better you get at it. This is a mixed bag, but think of life's challenges as opportunities for growth!

Don't get discouraged if life offers you opportunity after opportunity to use your discernment. Your unstoppable Father is offering you chance after chance to grow, stretch, and develop that discernment so that it comes naturally from now on.

Thank You for solid food, Lord! I feel like I've been in a dress rehearsal for something big, but You're growing me into a woman of remarkable discernment, and I'm so grateful. Amen.

LOVE ABOUNDS WITH DISCERNMENT

And it is my prayer that your love may abound more and more,
with knowledge and all discernment, so that you may approve what
is excellent, and so be pure and blameless for the day of Christ.
PHILIPPIANS 1:9–10 ESV

What do love and discernment have to do with each other? Interesting question, right? They don't seem to be connected at all, and yet they are. We are called to love all people, even those we disagree with. But wisdom comes into play when you're able to discern that some of the ones you love are more complicated than others.

Why is this so important? Because "loving" doesn't necessarily mean binding yourself to someone. There are some folks we're never meant to link arms with—and that's okay. (Hey, you can love folks from a distance too!)

It's for your own protection that God often separates you from those you love. Don't fight it when those seasons come. Trust that He has something better, not just for you, but for that other person as well.

Lord, I get it. I can love from a distance. I don't always have
to be BFFs with everyone, especially not the ones who might
zap me of my strength. Thanks for Your discernment! Amen.

HIS WORD DISCERNS OUR THOUGHTS

For the word of God is living and active, sharper than any two-edged sword, piercing to the division of soul and of spirit, of joints and of marrow, and discerning the thoughts and intentions of the heart.

HEBREWS 4:12 ESV

Did you realize that the Word of God is alive and active? It's true! The Bible isn't just a random book that was written thousands of years ago. It still penetrates the hearts of believers, even now. It goes to the deep, dark places! The Word shines a light on your thoughts as well as on the deepest recesses of your heart.

When you read the Bible, when you stumble across the verses like the one from Hebrews 4:12, you realize that God can see straight inside your thoughts. And He has verses already prepared to help guide your straying thoughts back to where they need to be. It's fascinating to realize that He knew what you would be thinking even before you thought it. (Crazy, right?!)

Because God's Word is alive, it can change you inside and out. And once you are changed, you shine as a beacon for all your friends and loved ones to be changed as well. So open that Bible, girl! Get ready for the mirror of His Word!

Your Word speaks to me, Lord! It's unstoppable in the way it changes me—my thoughts, my heart, even my actions. Thank You for giving me this precious guide, Father! Amen.

DISCERNING GOD'S WILL

*Do not be conformed to this world, but be transformed by the
renewal of your mind, that by testing you may discern what
is the will of God, what is good and acceptable and perfect.*

ROMANS 12:2 ESV

God reveals His will in a number of ways: through the verses in the
Bible, by speaking quietly to your heart, by thrusting you into circumstances that force you to ask, "What's going on here, Lord?" And
all the while, He asks you to keep an open heart and mind so that
you're 100 percent sure the messages you're hearing are from Him.

Why does He care so much about this? Because the world is
throwing all kinds of messages your way, and boy, are they chaotic!
You see them on social media. You hear them on the evening news.
Hollywood adds their spin. Your neighbors and friends share their
thoughts—loudly. Even churches can't agree on what message should
be preached. (Ouch!) The voices come at you hard and fast. Sometimes
it's hard to know who—or what—to believe.

But you can discern God's voice through it all. You really can. It
might seem impossible, but your unstoppable heavenly Father delights
in the impossible! Once you hear His voice more clearly, you can
discern His will in a given situation. So, ears open! Eyes open! Have
unstoppable discernment, girl!

*Lord, I get it! You're asking me to use godly discernment so that I don't
miss You or confuse the voices of this world with Your voice. Help me
to keep my heart and ears in tune so that I always recognize Your
voice. Only then will I fully be able to discern Your will. Amen.*

SHE'S NOT GOING TO
GET IT. . .BUT YOU WILL

*But people who aren't spiritual can't receive these truths from God's
Spirit. It all sounds foolish to them and they can't understand it, for
only those who are spiritual can understand what the Spirit means.*

1 CORINTHIANS 2:14 NLT

Here's a hard truth, girl: not everyone is going to understand the things
of God. Your unsaved friends? They might actually think you're a little
bit nuts for some of your beliefs. They might even call you names or
ostracize you, push you out of their circle. This can hurt. A lot.

Why don't they understand His Word the way you do? Why
don't they see the things that are so glaringly obvious to you? Because
they were not born again of His Spirit. Discernment comes through
walking with the Spirit of God. He whispers things in the ears of
believers, and those who are not believers are simply not getting those
same messages. They're missing out more than they realize.

You can't blame a blind man for being blind. The same is true with
those who aren't born of God's Spirit. You can't force them to see what
they truly cannot see. The only answer is for them to be spiritually
awakened. Pray that they will come to know God. It's the only way
they will ever hear the same messages you are hearing in your spirit.

*Lord, thank You for speaking to me. Spirit of God, I welcome Your voice!
I long to hear more so that I can walk more closely with You. Please
bring new life to my friends so they can hear Your voice too. Amen.*

TEST EVERYTHING

Test everything; hold fast what is good.
1 THESSALONIANS 5:21 ESV

Are you a gullible girl? Do you fall for every joke? Do you get taken advantage of a lot? Do people tend to walk on you? If so, listen up! God wants to give you discernment so that you can rise above all those things. You won't be the brunt of jokes any longer if your eyes are wide open.

Why is spiritual discernment so important in this day and age? Not everyone is who they say they are. Not every situation is what it appears to be. (Hey, we even see this in the media and on the internet!) If you fall for every little thing, then you will stand for nothing.

So open your eyes of understanding. Listen closely to what God is speaking to your heart. Only then, as you test everything, will the truth of your unstoppable heavenly Father shine through the cacophony of voices.

I don't want to be gullible, Lord. I don't want to fall for lies or deception. I want to be discerning, to hear Your voice so clearly that I only follow after You and nothing or no one else. May I be unstoppable in testing every person, every situation, and every message so that I don't fall into deception! Amen.

NOT WHO THEY SAY THEY ARE

These people are false apostles. They are deceitful workers who disguise themselves as apostles of Christ. But I am not surprised! Even Satan disguises himself as an angel of light. So it is no wonder that his servants also disguise themselves as servants of righteousness. In the end they will get the punishment their wicked deeds deserve.

2 CORINTHIANS 11:13–15 NLT

It happened again. You saw a post on social media about a pastor caught up in a big scandal. Maybe he had an affair. Or perhaps he was doing something immoral with his finances—misusing contributions people gave to the church. (Hey, nothing surprises you these days!)

Here's a hard truth, girl: not everyone is who they say they are. Even some of the ones who stand up in front of a church are leading double lives. This is one reason why you have to be so discerning. Don't fall for their tricks.

The same is true with some of your Christian friends. Not all of them are living the life they claim to have in Jesus. Some are double minded and trying to deceive others by pretending to be something they are not. But you? You're onto them. And you're doing everything you can to live in purity as you discern good from bad. Your unstoppable God wants you to remember that He has placed a calling on you to live a holy life. You can do it, girl!

This isn't easy, Lord! I want to believe everyone. I want to trust everyone! But it's so hard when people are being deceptive. Thank You for giving me discernment so that I can tell the fakers from the real deal. Amen.

SURROUNDED BY WOLVES

"Behold, I am sending you out as sheep in the midst of wolves, so be wise as serpents and innocent as doves."

MATTHEW 10:16 ESV

Wow! Take a look at today's verse. Jesus is sending us out as sheep in the midst of wolves. We're surrounded on every side by would-be attackers. No pressure!

No wonder we need to have our guard up! No wonder we need spiritual discernment so much. No wonder He tells us to be wise as serpents and innocent as doves. If it's true that some of the people around us are leading double lives (deceiving many with their pious acts), then we have to be ready to do battle.

How do we do that? On our knees, of course! We have to be ready to engage in spiritual warfare, to combat the fakers and even the ones who vocally (and often vehemently) oppose our faith. By separating ourselves from those who oppose us, not giving in to the temptation to become more like them. (Hint: that's just what the enemy of your soul wants, for you to be drawn to the wrong crowd.)

Be wise. Be discerning. Keep your distance. And pray as never before!

Lord, I get it. Sometimes I really feel like a lonely little sheep in a field of wolves! They're noisy. They're angry. And they don't like what I stand for, so they want to take me down. But I'm onto them! You're more powerful than all of them put together, my unstoppable God! So I won't give in to fear. Amen.

DON'T BE TAKEN CAPTIVE!

See to it that no one takes you captive by philosophy and empty deceit, according to human tradition, according to the elemental spirits of the world, and not according to Christ.

COLOSSIANS 2:8 ESV

They want to win you over with their beliefs, their ideologies. They have persuasive arguments. They're not willing to quit sharing them either. They're loud. They're aggressive. And they're everywhere—all over social media, on the news channels, and even in advertising! And boy, do people flock to them. Even Christians are changing their beliefs to become more like the world.

But not you. You've made up your mind. You won't be taken captive. These folks won't grab hold of your thoughts or take away your beliefs. No way! Their human understanding doesn't begin to compare to the things you've learned while walking with Jesus. His Spirit has poured out discernment, understanding, and revelation about this current age. And you're not going to get sucked down any rabbit hole.

Unstoppable discernment has saved you from captivity, girl! It's a gift from your unstoppable God. Today, pause to thank Him for sparing you the pain of falling into the enemy's trap!

Lord, thank You for sparing me! It's only because of Your discernment that I haven't fallen prey to the enemy's schemes. I won't become like the world. I will remain set apart! Amen.

UNSTOPPABLE TRUST

*Trust in the LORD with all your heart and
lean not on your own understanding.*

PROVERBS 3:5 NIV

Who can you trust? These days you're always on your guard against the untrustworthy! Phishing emails. Fake news. Hyped-up advertising. The world is filled with fibbers (or exaggerators). And you've fallen for their schemes a time or two. Now you're left wondering, *Who in the world can I trust?*

Honestly? No one. Well, no one in the world anyway. The only One you can truly trust is your unstoppable God. He wants you to have unstoppable trust, not in the things of this world, but in Him! When you place your trust wholly and squarely on the only One who can truly be trusted with your heart, you will never fail.

Trust in Him on the good days. Trust in Him on the bad days. Watch as He performs His Word. He's really great at keeping His promises, after all! You will witness miracles if you don't give up, if your trust is well placed on the Creator of all. (And while you're at it, don't fall for those crazy email schemes, girl!)

*I could put my trust in so many things, Lord. My finances.
My job. My family. Even my own abilities. But I will surely
fail if I don't place my trust squarely in You. Thank You
for that reminder, my unstoppable heavenly Father.*

137

I WILL NOT BE AFRAID

When I am afraid, I put my trust in you. In God, whose word I praise, in God I trust; I shall not be afraid. What can flesh do to me?

PSALM 56:3–4 ESV

Take a close look at the title of today's devotion. Can you say those words and mean them? Is it really possible to live a life free from fear?

The only way you can make strides in this direction is by wholly and completely putting your trust in God. You will begin to fall the moment you take your eyes off Him. Think of the story of the disciple Peter, who tried to walk on water toward Jesus. When he looked at his own abilities, he started to sink. But while he focused on the Savior? He stayed on top!

If you put your trust in your circumstances or your own abilities, the outcome will not be a good one. You'll be like Peter when he looked away from Jesus—you'll start to sink! And that sinking feeling brings with it a tremendous amount of fear. When you place your trust in anything *other* than the Lord, your knees will knock and your hands will tremble. Why? Because everything else is shaky ground. He's the only solid Rock, and you need to cling to Him, girl! Then fear will dispel because He's capable of keeping you afloat.

Lord, I will not be afraid. I will keep my eyes on You.
Like Peter walking across the sea, I won't lose my focus.
I don't have to be afraid as long as I stick with You. Amen.

YOUR TRUST, HIS ACTIONS

Commit your way to the LORD; trust in him and he will
do this: He will make your righteous reward shine like
the dawn, your vindication like the noonday sun.

PSALM 37:5–6 NIV

God's way is usually the polar opposite of our own. When something goes wrong, we want to jump right in headfirst and fix it. But take a look at today's scripture. God wants your trust. In fact, the next part of the verse seems to imply that your trust in Him activates His response. You place your trust in your unstoppable God and He flies into action. He fixes the problem. See how opposite that is from human nature?

Your precious heavenly Father has His own way of doing things, but it all begins with one very simple word: *trust*. Not yourself, not your actions, but in Him, fully and completely. So commit your way to Him. No, really. Make that commitment. Then watch as He takes the ball and runs with it.

I like to dive right into a problem, Lord. I'm a fix-it-yourselfer.
But You? You have a better way. So I place my trust in You, not in my
own actions. May You be activated by my faith, my unstoppable God.

TRUST IN HIS LOVE

I have trusted in your steadfast love;
my heart shall rejoice in your salvation.

PSALM 13:5 ESV

Think about the most trustworthy people you know. How do you know you can place your trust in them? No doubt they have earned it because of their love for you. It's hard to trust someone who clearly doesn't care about you, after all.

This is how you know you can trust your unstoppable God! He has proven Himself trustworthy because of His great love for you. That love took Jesus all the way to the cross, where He gave Himself as a sacrifice for your sin. He was tortured and bled and died so that You could live forever. What other proof do you need that your unstoppable God will stop at nothing to prove His love for you?

Because of that great love, He has more than earned your trust. May your heart rejoice today as you contemplate the trustworthiness of your precious, loving heavenly Father!

Lord, You've proved Your love time and time again. You adore me! And because I sense Your love, I know I can place my trust in You. You'll never let me down, my unstoppable God! Amen.

PERFECT PEACE

*"You keep him in perfect peace whose mind is stayed
on you, because he trusts in you. Trust in the LORD
forever, for the LORD GOD is an everlasting rock."*

ISAIAH 26:3–4 ESV

Imagine this: You're facing a difficult situation—complex. Gut wrenching. And you're ready to give up. But then you sense God's presence. You're reminded that placing your trust in Him, your immovable, everlasting Rock, is the only way to get through this.

So you do it. Somehow, in the very middle of your pain, you shift your focus and place your trust in Him. And then, miraculously, peace floods over you. Inexplicable peace. Unimaginable peace. It descends like a cloud, bringing hope. And joy. And a sense of expectation you didn't have before.

Such is the power of trusting in your unstoppable God! He's your Rock, your Fortress, your Peace Giver. And He's keenly aware of what you're walking through, even now. Trust Him, sweet woman of God. You'll be so glad you did.

*Lord, thank You for that blanket of peace. It can be mine
when I place my trust in You. I choose to do that today,
even while walking through the valley. Amen.*

ACKNOWLEDGE HIM

Trust in the LORD with all your heart, and do not lean on your own understanding. In all your ways acknowledge him, and he will make straight your paths.

PROVERBS 3:5–6 ESV

Have you ever felt overlooked? Maybe you did something kind for someone but they didn't even give you a nod afterward. It's a terrible feeling, isn't it?

Don't you imagine God sometimes feels like that? He works on our behalf and we don't even acknowledge what He's done. He performs a miracle for a loved one and we go on with our lives as if nothing significant has happened.

Today's passage says that we are to trust Him with all our hearts and lean not on our own understanding. No doubt you've read that verse many times before. But check out the rest of it. "In all your ways acknowledge him, and he will make straight your paths."

Aha! To receive clear marching orders and for things to go smoothly, we have to acknowledge God in all our ways. Not just a few, but all! Take some time to do that today.

Lord, please forgive me for the times I forgot to acknowledge You! Without You, my unstoppable, trustworthy God, I'm nothing! I'll stumble and fall! My paths will be crooked. So I place my trust squarely in You, knowing that You will guide me every step of the way. Amen.

HE WON'T FORSAKE YOU

Those who know your name put their trust in you,
for you, O LORD, have not forsaken those who seek you.

PSALM 9:10 ESV

Imagine you put your trust in a loved one, say, a spouse, and then he abandoned you. You'd feel completely betrayed. Let down. And who could blame you? What a blow!

Here's the wonderful thing about your unstoppable, loving heavenly Father: He never forsakes those who seek Him. Others will, as you've no doubt experienced. But God? Never. Not even when you turn your back on Him. He won't give up on you. (You could test this theory all day, but He wins every time.)

Because you have the assurance that God won't forsake you, it's easy to put your trust in Him. (Let's face it, trusting those who love us is an easy task!) And God loves you ten thousand times more than you can possibly imagine, so you are safe with Him, girl! He will never leave you or forsake you.

Lord, I know I can trust You. I've given You plenty of reasons to turn
and walk away, and yet You never do! You're in this for the long haul.
I am too! Now that my trust is rooted in You, my unstoppable God,
I have the assurance that You are completely trustworthy! Amen.

A TREE PLANTED BY WATER

*"Blessed is the man who trusts in the LORD, whose trust is the LORD.
He is like a tree planted by water, that sends out its roots by the stream,
and does not fear when heat comes, for its leaves remain green, and is
not anxious in the year of drought, for it does not cease to bear fruit."*

JEREMIAH 17:7–8 ESV

Have you ever watched a large tree topple over in a storm? Perhaps its roots didn't run deep enough. A strong wind came along, and down it went.

God wants you to be like a tree with deep roots. He wants your trust in Him to be so deeply rooted that nothing—absolutely nothing—topples you.

Instead of looking to the world for answers, look to God. Allow your spiritual roots to go deep into His Word. Learn as much as you can. Glean wisdom. Hang out with godly people. Spend time in prayer. Before long, the depth of your relationship will have you so deeply rooted that even the strongest winds couldn't possibly send you toppling over!

*Lord, I don't want to waste a minute! I want my roots to
run deep. May I spend as much time as possible studying
Your Word, Your ways, and Your godly people. May my roots
run deeper and deeper with each passing day. Amen.*

A BETTER WAY

It is better to take refuge in the LORD than to trust in humans.

PSALM 118:8 NIV

You have your own way of doing things, don't you? The way you cook. The way you clean. The way you speak. The way you drive. You've settled into a routine, and it's comfortable to you. Heaven help the one who tries to change you!

When it comes to where you place your trust, God has a better way. No, really. He sees you trying to place trust in yourself. Or your loved ones. Or your bank account. He watches as you begin to trust in the politicians, the weatherman, even the media. But His way is always better—than yours or theirs!

You have a choice to make, woman of God! You can place your trust in the things of man or in the Creator of all. It's really that simple. Their way or His way. Their plans or His plans. God lets you choose, so choose wisely!

Lord, I choose You! I choose Your way, Your plan, Your actions. I'm done putting my trust in politicians, in the media, or even in myself. Talk about a lousy way to live! No, I'll shift my trust wholly and completely to You, my unstoppable, trustworthy God! Amen.

NOURISHMENT TO YOUR BONES

Do not be wise in your own eyes; fear the LORD and shun evil.
This will bring health to your body and nourishment to your bones.

PROVERBS 3:7–8 NIV

When you do things God's way, you'll receive great benefits. Some of them are spiritual (eternal life, leading others toward an eternal relationship with Him), and others are physical (health to your body and nourishment to your bones).

Following Jesus is a win-win on every level, isn't it? Why, then, do we so often put our trust in ourselves? Why do we allow ourselves to become captivated by the world's way of doing things? The so-called benefits of trusting man (as opposed to God) are pathetic! There's no health to our bodies when we're chasing after the things of this world, after all. There's no joy, no peace, no tranquility.

Today, be reminded that your unstoppable God wants you to do things His way—for your sake. The benefits are all for you! So don't be wise in your own eyes. Give up the world's way. Let God have His way, and watch as the blessings flow!

I get it, Jesus! You have nothing but good things for me when I place my trust in You. I'll do my best to do so in every area of my life. Amen.

UNSTOPPABLE HOPE

"For I know the plans I have for you, declares the LORD, plans for welfare and not for evil, to give you a future and a hope."
JEREMIAH 29:11 ESV

You are not without hope. Even in the deepest valley, shimmers of sunlight overhead remind you that God hasn't forsaken you. He has big plans for you, girl, and they are plans for good, not evil.

Stop to think that through. Your unstoppable God wants to give you unstoppable hope. Even when it feels like your proverbial ship is sinking. Even when you're facing a financial crisis or dealing with a sick child. Even then, you can have hope. How is this possible? By remembering what He has already brought you through.

The same God who carried you through the valleys of yesterday will lift you over the mountains of tomorrow. He has a future out there for you. And a hope. He has "welfare" (caring for your needs), not plans for evil. In other words, you can trust Him implicitly. Put your hope in your unstoppable, loving heavenly Father! Lean on Him today and anticipate a great tomorrow.

You have great plans for me, Lord! I'm filled with newfound hope as I think about all You have in store. Thank You, my unstoppable God! Amen.

BY THE POWER OF HIS SPIRIT

*May the God of hope fill you with all joy and peace in believing,
so that by the power of the Holy Spirit you may abound in hope.*

ROMANS 15:13 ESV

Just hoping for something is not enough. That hope has got to be undergirded with something very powerful. God has given you His Holy Spirit, and He comes with a megadose of power. So, as you activate your faith, as your hope grows, ask the Spirit of God to invigorate you with power from on high.

What are you hoping for? What impossible thing are you believing God for? (Hint: think big! He can handle it!) Ask for the wind of the Spirit to fill you. You'll be pleasantly surprised at what He can accomplish. After all, He can do all the things you cannot do!

God cares about the things you're hoping for. And He longs for you to trust Him fully. Give Him free rein to sweep in with His power from on high so that you can see miracles take place! Brace yourself, girl! Amazing things are coming!

Holy Spirit, breathe on this situation! Imbue me with heavenly power to believe for the impossible, to hope even when common sense says, "Just give up!" I won't give up, Lord! I'll be unstoppable in my quest to see these things come to pass. Amen.

THINGS NOT SEEN

Now faith is the assurance of things hoped for,
the conviction of things not seen.

HEBREWS 11:1 ESV

You haven't actually seen it yet. It hasn't come to pass. But in your spirit, you see it as plain as day. That miracle you're waiting on is as good as done in your mind.

People wonder why you're so confident about it. Some even question your sanity. But they don't understand how faith works. They don't get it. You have hope for the things you haven't seen yet because of that faith. In fact, you're completely convinced before you ever see the evidence.

What a fun and exciting way to live! What a faith journey this is. You are a woman who puts her trust in the One true God, and you have unstoppable hope for the future as a result.

Lord, I place my hope in You. I can't see the miracles yet, but they are coming. I can feel it. One day everyone will see what I see. Until then I'll keep my eyes and heart fixed on You! Amen.

IF YOU CAN SEE IT. . .IT'S NOT HOPE

We were given this hope when we were saved. (If we already have something, we don't need to hope for it. But if we look forward to something we don't yet have, we must wait patiently and confidently.)

ROMANS 8:24–25 NLT

What a fascinating scripture! And girl, it's true! If you can see it, it's not hope. Wow. Makes sense, though. It takes no faith to believe what you can see with your eyes, does it? But what about those things you can't see? Believing for the not-yet-visible takes more faith, for sure.

If you could see it, you wouldn't have the same sense of anticipation. But because you can't, you're waiting with bated breath! The excitement is building to a crescendo as you sense God working on your behalf. You're like a kid waiting for Christmas morning. You can envision what will be under that tree, and so your anticipation builds. And builds. And builds.

Your unstoppable God loves this sense of expectation that's rising up inside you. Nothing pleases Him more than a child who lives by faith!

May my hope be unstoppable, Lord! Thank You for the excitement that is building inside me even now. Amen.

HOPE IS ALIVE!

Blessed be the God and Father of our Lord Jesus Christ! According to his great mercy, he has caused us to be born again to a living hope through the resurrection of Jesus Christ from the dead.

1 PETER 1:3 ESV

Perhaps you've heard the phrase "Keep hope alive!" Can you really do that by yourself? Can you manufacture hope, or is it contingent on something else altogether?

Hope is a living, breathing thing. No doubt about that. But consider this: the only real hope comes from a supernatural encounter with your unstoppable God. He can infuse you with the pulse of hope, the heartbeat of hope, the promise of hope. And with that promise comes a great future! When you begin to view hope as a living, breathing thing, you see the potential, not just for the situation you're currently walking through, but for all the struggles yet to come.

You, sweet girl? You don't have the power in your pinkie finger to keep hope alive. Try all day. You can't drum it up. But here's a fun secret: it never died in the first place. It lives and breathes in the person of Jesus Christ, who was, who is, and who always will be. Hallelujah!

Thank You for planting hope in my heart, Lord. I feel its quickening. I sense its potential. Thank You, my unstoppable God. Amen.

WRITTEN DOWN FOR US

Such things were written in the Scriptures long ago to teach us. And the Scriptures give us hope and encouragement as we wait patiently for God's promises to be fulfilled.

ROMANS 15:4 NLT

Can you even imagine all the many, many years it took to write the Bible? So many men! So many experiences! So much revelation from their heavenly Father. (Wow!) And all of it so that we could enjoy the message of a loving Savior right here and right now in the twenty-first century.

The Bible is a living, breathing document. It's far more than a history book, much more than words on paper, penciled in haste. Your unstoppable God made sure it was written down so that you could have hope.

Think about that for a moment. If the Bible didn't exist, would you know God to the extent that you do? No way! Those verses lift your spirits when you're having a hard day and provide fresh insight and revelation into what you're going through. God knew the road you would walk and planned those verses just for you. Well, you—and billions of others too!

Thank You for giving us Your Word, Lord! The verses in the Bible give me such hope. Where would I be without them? I praise You for the unstoppable message found in the Bible! Amen.

FOR WHAT DO I WAIT?

"And now, O Lord, for what do I wait? My hope is in you."
PSALM 39:7 ESV

If you're like most women, you have a hard time waiting. No doubt you've proved this over the years. Many give up hope before they see the fulfillment of a dream. They hop off the bus before reaching their destination then wonder why they're lost on unfamiliar streets, feeling hopeless and alone. They give up just short of seeing the miracle take place.

But you? You're not giving up. Hope is pounding in your heart. You hear it resonating in your ears, a steady rhythm that keeps you going on even the toughest of days. You are committed to waiting because your faith is activated and it has brought with it great hope for a good future.

Pray for your friends and loved ones who are at the giving-up point. Pray for an infusion of hope from their heavenly Father so that they can keep waiting with joyous expectation, as you are, even now.

I'll keep waiting, Jesus! Hope is pounding in my heart.
How could I possibly give up now? I'll hang tight to You
and spread this hopeful message to all I meet. Amen.

CHRIST IN YOU, THE HOPE OF GLORY

*To them God chose to make known how great among
the Gentiles are the riches of the glory of this mystery,
which is Christ in you, the hope of glory.*

COLOSSIANS 1:27 ESV

Do you ever stop to think about what your life was like before you came to know Jesus? It's sobering to reminisce, isn't it?

Perhaps you tried to manufacture hope during hopeless seasons but never understood why it didn't fully work. Maybe you turned to others, praying they would offer hopeful words. Or you listened to sermons, hungry for hopeful messages. These are all good things, but without the infusion of the Holy Spirit, those messages won't stick!

When Christ came to live in your heart, everything changed! He brought the wind of the Spirit of God! Christ is the hope of glory. With Jesus, you don't even have to try. He simply is.

This is one reason why it's so important to get the Gospel message out. Around this globe, people are facing hopeless situations. Without a genuine relationship with the Savior of the world, how will they survive? They need Christ, the hope of glory. Will you be the one to share the message?

*I will tell them, Lord! I'll share Your message of hope
with all I meet! This world can be turned around with
an infusion of God-inspired hope! Amen.*

HOPE WON'T MAKE YOU ASHAMED

*Hope never makes us ashamed because the love of
God has come into our hearts through the Holy
Spirit Who was given to us. We were weak and
could not help ourselves. Then Christ came at the
right time and gave His life for all sinners.*

ROMANS 5:5–6 NLV

You have probably had many times in your life when you messed up. Made poor choices. No doubt you came out of those experiences riddled with shame. You couldn't hold up your head to look God in the eye. Like Adam in the garden, you shifted your gaze to the ground.

Here's one piece of good news today: hope in Christ will never leave you ashamed. When you place your trust squarely in Him and not yourself, there's always a good outcome. Oh, people might wonder why you keep hanging on, believing for something that feels impossible. But that unstoppable hope will not disappoint you. You won't be left riddled with shame as a result of your faith. Just the opposite, in fact. You will be energized and boosted as hope remains very much alive in your heart.

And here's more good news: hope is contagious! Before long, everyone will want what you have. So hang in there, sister! Don't give up on what could be the brink of a miracle!

*Thank You for the infusion of Your Holy Spirit,
my unstoppable God. I know that the hope You have
placed in my heart will never leave me ashamed.*

THE WEIGHT OF GLORY

So we do not lose heart. Though our outer self is wasting away, our inner self is being renewed day by day. For this light momentary affliction is preparing for us an eternal weight of glory beyond all comparison, as we look not to the things that are seen but to the things that are unseen. For the things that are seen are transient, but the things that are unseen are eternal.

2 CORINTHIANS 4:16–18 ESV

The human body ages moment by moment, day by day, year by year. Perhaps you look in the mirror and groan because your physique has changed so much from days gone by. Let's face it—wrinkles appear, skin sags, certain body parts don't look the way they once did. Far from it, in fact!

And yet the inner man is stronger than ever. Fascinating, right? When your unstoppable God infuses you with supernatural hope, your spirit man remains very much alive. Energized. Healthy. Strong. Age doesn't matter! Some of the strongest believers on the planet are senior citizens. Many are toughened by their years of walking with the Lord. They're stronger than ever on the inside!

Don't be discouraged by what you see on the outside, girl. Remember, in heaven you're going to get a new body anyway. But that spirit? It's still going strong! Now that's something to celebrate!

Thank You for the hope that keeps my inner self healthy and well, Jesus. The exterior is in a state of flux, but I am unstoppable from the inside out. Keep growing me into a woman of internal fortitude and strength! Amen.

A SAFE ANCHOR FOR OUR SOULS

God gave these two things that cannot be changed and God cannot lie. We who have turned to Him can have great comfort knowing that He will do what He has promised. This hope is a safe anchor for our souls. It will never move. This hope goes into the Holiest Place of All behind the curtain of heaven.

HEBREWS 6:18–19 NLV

Picture a boat tied to the pier. A storm comes along and pulls it loose from its moorings. Off it goes, drifting out to sea.

In many ways, people are like that little boat. Many are barely hanging on, easily pulled this way and that because they're not truly anchored to anything. The believer, however? She's anchored to her Rock, Jesus. She's not going anywhere! She has the hope of her salvation and the comfort that He's holding tight to her. She's not worried about being pulled out to sea.

Sweet woman of God, your unstoppable heavenly Father won't let you go. He'll keep your hope alive even if the waves come. Take comfort. You're not going anywhere!

Thank You for holding tight to me, my unstoppable God! I have such hope because I know You will never, ever let me go. I'm safe with You, and that makes my heart so happy! Amen.

UNSTOPPABLE POWER

This is the last thing I want to say: Be strong with the Lord's strength. Put on the things God gives you to fight with. Then you will not fall into the traps of the devil.

EPHESIANS 6:10–11 NLV

Your unstoppable God wants to fill you with strength and might! Stop and read those words again. *Your unstoppable God wants to fill you with strength and might*! He wants you to be overflowing with power to face any obstacle!

So what does that look like? How does it play out in the real world? Are you supposed to go to the gym and build up those muscles until you look like Samson or Goliath? Will a new diet help? Maybe some supplements? Or is this a different kind of strength altogether?

It's great to have physical strength, but spiritual fortitude is even more vital. God wants you to be strong enough that when you come up against temptation you don't fall into the enemy's trap. He wants you to be tough enough that you can say no to the things you need to say no to. Most of all, He wants you to be strong in your time spent with Him. Nothing you face can take you down when you're infused with His unstoppable power from on high. You are a woman of strength!

Thank You for making me strong and mighty, Lord. I don't always feel it, but I trust that You are doing a powerful work inside me. Amen.

IT'S HIS GREATNESS

*"O Lord, You have great power, shining-greatness and strength.
Yes, everything in heaven and on earth belongs to You. You are
the King, O Lord. And You are honored as head over all."*

1 CHRONICLES 29:11 NLV

Some women are happy to show off their "heavenly" strengths. They want the world to think they are spiritual powerhouses. Some of them strut their stuff in front of the masses. They lead Bible studies or teach large groups of women in public settings. But then you find out they are living a completely different kind of life behind the scenes. Or maybe they go public with messages that are contrary to the Gospel. Ouch!

God is far more interested in authenticity. And remember, it's not your strength anyway. If you're going to shine a light on anything at all, then shine it on Him! Shine it on His greatness. Shine it on His ability to take care of this wonderful, terrible, broken world. Shine it on His power to save, to deliver, and to heal. He is King of all and deserves the spotlight!

May the strength that God gives never make you arrogant or pious. Don't get caught in the enemy's sneaky trap. May God's unstoppable strength only ever drive you back to Him.

*I want to shine Your light brightly, Jesus! May people
never look at me or my accomplishments. May they
only see You shining brightly through me. Amen.*

HIS POWER IS WORKING

Now to him who is able to do far more abundantly than all that we ask or think, according to the power at work within us.
EPHESIANS 3:20 ESV

Your unstoppable God never quits. He's on the clock 24-7. He can do far more than you could ever imagine. In fact, today's verse says He can do abundantly more than you could ask or think. Wow!

And here's the really cool part: even when you're sound asleep at night, God is still working. When you're half-awake the next morning? He's already on the job. And when you're frustrated with the way your day is going, He already has plans in motion for tomorrow. He simply never quits. And His unstoppable power is working inside you through all of that.

When you realize that your unstoppable God works around the clock, does it build confidence? Morning, noon, or night He adores You and will care for your every need, girl. So don't fret! Just relax and trust Him!

> *Thank You for staying on the clock, Lord! Your power is unstoppable. Your love and dedication to me go beyond my wildest imaginings. Thank You, thank You! Amen.*

WITH HIM, YOU CAN!

I know how to get along with little and how to live when I have much.
I have learned the secret of being happy at all times. If I am full of
food and have all I need, I am happy. If I am hungry and need more,
I am happy. I can do all things because Christ gives me the strength.

PHILIPPIANS 4:12–13 NLV

Picture yourself at the gym trying to lift several hundred pounds. By yourself, you could never do it. Not a chance. You wouldn't even get those weights off the ground. Now picture your trainer standing in front of you, his hands also gripping the weights. Together you begin to lift. And then you realize that he's actually the one carrying the brunt of the weight.

Such is the case when you walk with Jesus! He takes those burdens, He takes those trials, and He lifts them as if they are light as a feather. To Him, they are! What seems impossible to you is completely doable for your powerful, unstoppable God. Sure, you'll still go through things. You'll have lean seasons and seasons of plenty. But through it all, He'll be right there, doing the lifting.

You really can do all things through Him who strengthens you, girl. Really!

I get it, Lord! By myself, I cannot. But with You, I can!
How grateful I am to You, my heavy lifter! Amen.

ONCE GOD HAS SPOKEN

God has spoken once. I have heard this twice: Power belongs to God.
PSALM 62:11 NLV

The words God speaks over your situation have tremendous power. You might feel down in the dumps, but He says you are an overcomer. You might feel weak, but He says You are strong. You might be ill, but He says that you are healed by the stripes He bore on His body at Calvary. His words matter, and they carry power like you can't even imagine! (Remember, this is the same God who spoke the world into existence!)

Words have power, and that power belongs to your unstoppable heavenly Father. But God is definitely interested in how and what you speak over your situation too! He longs for you to speak words of life and hope, even in the toughest circumstances. Your words have the power to heal, to change, and to shift circumstances. Wow!

So keep your focus, woman of God! The words you speak have strength and power. You can (literally) lift your own spirits just by changing how you speak. Ready to see change in your life? Speak it, girl!

Lord, I don't always speak positive things over my life.
I get weary and my words become negative. Thank You
for the reminder that the spoken word has power! Amen.

POWER TO WITNESS

"You will receive power when the Holy Spirit has come upon you, and you will be my witnesses in Jerusalem and in all Judea and Samaria, and to the end of the earth."

ACTS 1:8 ESV

Why do you suppose the enemy of your soul works so hard to bring you down? Why attack your health or your emotions? Could it be that he is trying to stop you from spreading the Gospel? After all, it's hard to be a good witness when you're feeling subpar. He's banking on that, in fact!

Here's the deal: God has given you power from the Holy Spirit. Why? So that you can be a witness locally (your home, family, job, and city) and beyond! You can impact your friends, family, and coworkers right where you are, but you can also impact the lives of friends on the social media mission field, girl! (And who knows—maybe you'll end up going on a mission trip too!)

Stay strong—internally and externally! Let the Spirit of God invigorate you for the tasks ahead! You really do have the power to be an effective witness if you'll stay the course.

Thank You for the reminder that You want me to be strong for a reason, Lord! I'm to be a powerhouse for You so that I can spread the Gospel message. Thank You for power to do the work! Amen.

THE POWER FOR SALVATION

I am not ashamed of the Good News. It is the power of God. It is the way He saves men from the punishment of their sins if they put their trust in Him. It is for the Jew first and for all other people also.

ROMANS 1:16 NLV

Have you ever paused to think about how powerful the Gospel message really is? In an instant, that message can change a heart for all eternity. It can take a drug addict and bring about complete deliverance. It can take an angry, abusive spouse and put a cease and desist order in his tumultuous heart. It can take a woman on the brink of suicide and bring her back from the abyss.

Talk about supernatural, unstoppable power! And all of it can be yours in an instant as you accept Jesus as your Savior. Wow!

The Gospel message, if shared across this globe in its fullness, would eradicate sin, would heal broken hearts, and would bring about world peace. No wonder the enemy works so hard to stop that message from getting out! We must not be ashamed of the Gospel, for it is truly the most powerful weapon we believers have. Keep proclaiming it, girl! Think about the lives you can help change!

Thank You, Jesus, for the power to see lives changed.
Your work on the cross accomplished everything we
could ever need and more. How grateful I am. Amen.

WEAK THEN STRONG

For he was crucified in weakness, but lives by the power
of God. For we also are weak in him, but in dealing
with you we will live with him by the power of God.

2 CORINTHIANS 13:4 ESV

Jesus was crucified when His physical body was at its absolute weakest, but He later rose from the dead, a full demonstration of the power of God. He moved from weak to strong.

Likewise, you go through weak periods. You feel as vulnerable as a newborn babe, crushed by the circumstances swirling around you. You wonder if you'll ever feel powerful again. Then a new season comes along and things are better. You feel more hopeful. You're invigorated and feeling stronger than before.

These hills and valleys are completely normal for the believer. If you lived on the mountaintop all the time, you couldn't experience what it means to have to trust Him in the valleys. So don't fight the weak, weary seasons. Just remember that better days are coming. Before long you'll feel strong once again.

I won't fight the seasons, Lord. I'll remind myself that You are
stronger. I'll remind myself that tomorrow will be better. Thank You
for taking me from the valley to the mountaintop, Lord! Amen.

HIS DIVINE POWER

His divine power has granted to us all things that
pertain to life and godliness, through the knowledge
of him who called us to his own glory and excellence.

2 PETER 1:3 ESV

By yourself you don't have the power to live a godly life. No doubt you've already figured that out on your own! Oh, you've tried. You've followed the rules. You've tried to behave. You've done well for a while and then taken a tumble. You've slipped up. You've fallen more times than you can count. Hey, you're human! Still, the whole process feels grueling.

What you cannot accomplish with all your good works Jesus has already accomplished through His divine power. He has granted everything that you could ever need to lead a good, godly life. He did it through His work on the cross. And He did it because He's calling you to glory and to excellence. So don't beat yourself up! Just settle into what He has already provided. Rest assured in the fact that He has taken care of everything you cannot.

Thank You for Your divine power, giving me life and godliness.
Without You, I am powerless. When I place my trust in
You, nothing is impossible! How grateful I am! Amen.

UNSTOPPABLE PROVISION

And God is able to make all grace abound to you,
so that having all sufficiency in all things at all
times, you may abound in every good work.

2 CORINTHIANS 9:8 ESV

Your unstoppable God stands ready to provide all you could possibly need to make it through this life. He has finances to make sure your bills are paid. He has emotional strength when you're going through a tough time. He has healing power when you're not feeling well.

The Lord wants you to have all you need. Stop to think about that for a moment. There's no lack in God's house. He won't leave you stranded! Sure, there might be lean seasons, but even then He will make provision. (Hasn't He always done so in the past, girl? Why do you fret?)

What do you need today? Food? Shelter? A new job? Friendships? A nudge to lose weight? Supernatural courage? Your unstoppable God wants to hear from you about those things. He will provide in ways that exceed your expectations! Why? So that you are freed up to do the work He has called you to do, of course! (Hey, it's hard to work when you're hungry or distressed!)

Thank You for meeting all my needs, Lord!
I'm grateful for Your provision in all areas of my
life—physical, emotional, and psychological. Amen.

HIS RICHES IN GLORY

*My God will supply every need of yours according
to his riches in glory in Christ Jesus.*

PHILIPPIANS 4:19 ESV

No doubt there have been seasons of your life when you felt like a pauper. Maybe you pictured yourself going to the King of kings, hands extended, asking for a crust of bread. You wondered if He would come through for you, but He always did!

Here's the cool thing about your unstoppable God: He owns the cattle on a thousand hills. He's richer than any corporate executive! And He has promised to meet all your needs, not out of your storehouse (or your provision) but out of His own riches.

Whoa. The One who owns the cattle on a thousand hills wants to make sure your rent is paid? Wants to assure you that your children will have all they need? Wants to provide groceries and money for car payments. . .and everything else too? Yes, He does!

Before you panic over your financial situation, remind yourself that the One who owns it all sees your need and has promised to provide.

*You're unstoppable in Your provision, Lord! Your storehouses
are full, and You're so generous to share with Your children.
I'll do my best not to doubt but to trust. Amen.*

THE RIGHTEOUS WILL NEVER BE FORSAKEN

I have been young, and now am old, yet I have not seen the righteous forsaken or his children begging for bread. He is ever lending generously, and his children become a blessing.

PSALM 37:25–26 ESV

Think about when you were a kid, how your mom sent you to your room without your supper after you sassed her. God doesn't operate like that. No matter what, He makes sure you have the provision you need. Your unstoppable heavenly Father will never leave His kids begging for bread. What a relief, right?

Of course, it doesn't always feel like it in the moment. Like that time you didn't have the rent money or that other time when you were short on groceries. But remember how He swept in and proved Himself, right in the middle of your panic attack? A random check appeared in the mailbox. He helped you roll the payment on the loan. A miracle took place to see you through.

God has always been there for you, and He won't leave you now. Your unstoppable God cares deeply about you and will never forsake you.

Thank You for Your provision, Lord! You're unstoppable in how You meet my needs. I'm grateful for Your tender, loving care! Amen.

ALL THESE THINGS

*"Seek first the kingdom of God and his righteousness,
and all these things will be added to you."*

MATTHEW 6:33 ESV

God's Word promises that if we will seek first His kingdom and His righteousness that all "these" things will be added to us. "All *what* things?" you ask.

Well. . .what do you need? Are you in need of financial provision? Do you need a miracle in your health? Are you believing for a broken relationship to be mended? Are you lonely and in need of a friend? God can handle all these things and more—emotional, physical, and even financial needs—with ease.

No matter what your need might be, God can meet it. But there is a side note! You have to seek Him. Diligently. With your whole heart. With your strength. You have to lay down your own wants and wishes long enough to put Him first. When He has His proper place, then all the things you lack can easily be added to your life.

*I get it, Lord! I put You first, and You turn around and make
my needs a priority. Help me focus on You, my unstoppable
God! Then I can truly witness miracles. Amen.*

NO MATTER WHAT YOU'RE FACING

I am not saying I need anything. I have learned to be happy
with whatever I have. I know how to get along with little
and how to live when I have much. I have learned the secret
of being happy at all times. If I am full of food and have all I
need, I am happy. If I am hungry and need more, I am happy.

PHILIPPIANS 4:11–12 NLV

Contentment is a choice, and it's something you must choose every day of your life. There are days when you need to choose joy even if you don't feel like it. There are days when you need to choose hope even when your hope is fading. But you can do it, girl. No, really, you can. Through Him all things are possible.

Contentment is the key to thriving under God's provision. No matter what situation you're in—whether it's a low low or a high high, contentment is the secret ingredient. It will help you understand God's abundance and His willingness to meet your needs.

What do you need today? Instead of moaning and groaning over your lack, begin to praise God. Then settle into contentment, knowing He already has you covered.

Lord, please forgive me for the times when I've been outwardly
(and inwardly) discontent. Sometimes I'm a grumbling mess.
Instead of seeing the good, I see only the bad. But You, Lord?
You remind me that with You, all of it is good. Amen.

HE KNOWS YOUR NEED

"Ask, and it will be given to you; seek, and you will find; knock, and it will be opened to you. For everyone who asks receives, and the one who seeks finds, and to the one who knocks it will be opened. Or which one of you, if his son asks him for bread, will give him a stone? Or if he asks for a fish, will give him a serpent? If you then, who are evil, know how to give good gifts to your children, how much more will your Father who is in heaven give good things to those who ask him!"

MATTHEW 7:7–11 ESV

What a marvelous passage! Your heavenly Father knows exactly what you need when you need it. And He's unstoppable in His quest to meet your needs. But be aware: sometimes what you think you need and what you actually need are two different things! (Aren't you glad your unstoppable God knows what's best?)

Ask. Seek. Knock. God is going to make provision. But His gifts might just supersede what you're asking for. No kidding! You might ask for rent money and He might come back with a new job. (Hey, He's pretty amazing like that!) You might ask for a good meal for your kids and He might give you an unexpected gift card from a loved one to your favorite restaurant. (Yum!)

Here's the point: whatever you ask for, He has you covered—and then some. He's a great gift giver!

Lord, thank You for giving me all I need and more! You truly know what I'm needing, even when I don't know how to ask. You give such good gifts, Father! How grateful I am. Amen.

HIS GOOD PLEASURE

"But seek his kingdom, and these things will be given to you as well. Do not be afraid, little flock, for your Father has been pleased to give you the kingdom. Sell your possessions and give to the poor. Provide purses for yourselves that will not wear out, a treasure in heaven that will never fail, where no thief comes near and no moth destroys. For where your treasure is, there your heart will be also."

LUKE 12:31–34 NIV

You've been there. You purchased a gift for a friend, the perfect-for-her item. You could hardly wait to give it to her! Seeing her reaction was priceless. The minute her eyes lit up, you knew you'd hit that nail on the head. How great you both felt!

God hits the nail on the head every single time. He knows you so well! And how fun to learn that He actually loves to bless you. (Hey, He's a good, good Father!) It's His good pleasure to give you the kingdom. Just like it's your pleasure to bless those you love.

Isn't that how life works, after all? When we love, we bless. (Who do you think you learned that from, if not from your unstoppable God?)

Oh, how He loves you. Oh, how He longs to pour out blessings in your life—so many that you can't contain them!

Lord, thank You! You show Your love for me with every sunrise. You meet my needs, even going above and beyond. How I praise You for Your unstoppable provision! Amen.

GIVE FREELY

*One gives freely, yet grows all the richer; another withholds
what he should give, and only suffers want. Whoever
brings blessing will be enriched, and one who waters will
himself be watered. The people curse him who holds back
grain, but a blessing is on the head of him who sells it.*

PROVERBS 11:24–26 ESV

God's math doesn't always make sense, does it? Give away 10 percent
of your income and you end up having more than you started with.
Have a heart to bless others (give, give, and give some more) and you're
the one who receives the blessing. It's almost upside down, isn't it?

Here's a fun truth: when you love others, you can't wait to bless
them. And when you water a garden, you end up reaping the harvest.
You can't help but be blessed when you "water" the people you love.
You'll produce a great crop, for sure!

Test God in this and see if He doesn't prove it! Give freely. Watch
Him meet your needs. Bring blessings—with your words, your actions,
your money—and your life will be enriched. That's just how your
unstoppable God works, girl!

*Lord, I get it! I don't give to get, but You always respond to my giving
by blessing me. I can't lose! Show me how. Show me who. Show me
when. I can't wait to get started with this "giving" lifestyle. Amen.*

THE FIRST WILL BE LAST

Peter began to say to [Jesus], "See, we have left everything and followed you." Jesus said, "Truly, I say to you, there is no one who has left house or brothers or sisters or mother or father or children or lands, for my sake and for the gospel, who will not receive a hundredfold now in this time, houses and brothers and sisters and mothers and children and lands, with persecutions, and in the age to come eternal life. But many who are first will be last, and the last first."

MARK 10:28–31 ESV

Some things in life make no sense to you. Wicked people get away with, well, everything! And many of them prosper financially while you struggle to pay the bills. (What's up with that, Lord?)

Here's an interesting truth from the Word of God: the first will be last and the last will be first. The very ones who seem to have it all in this life will end up losing it all when they don't make eternity. And those who struggle? Many of them will be blessed beyond measure.

Yes, you will be persecuted in this life. And yes, you may have scary moments when you wonder if God has forgotten you. (Hint: He hasn't!) But remember, there's coming a day when you will walk down streets of gold in eternity. He's there now, preparing a mansion with your name on it. Wouldn't you rather have that than all the cash in the world, after all?

Lord, I don't always understand why some people seem to have it all and others struggle to make ends meet. But I trust You, and I know heaven will be better than earth by far. Amen.

175

UNSTOPPABLE PROVISION

He spread a cloud for a covering, and fire to give light by night. They asked, and he brought quail, and gave them bread from heaven in abundance. He opened the rock, and water gushed out; it flowed through the desert like a river.

PSALM 105:39–41 ESV

God has always been in the provision business. Don't believe it? Check out a familiar story from the Old Testament. Think of the Israelites crossing the desert. How do you feed that many people? How do you provide enough water to sustain them? And yet that's exactly what your unstoppable God did! During the day He covered them with a cloud. At night He came in with a fire to give light. (He truly thought of everything!) When they were hungry, He gave quail. Thirsty? Water from a rock! And talk about showing off! He didn't just cause that water to trickle—it flowed through the desert like a river!

That's your unstoppable God at work. What makes you think He won't take care of your needs? If He can pull water from a rock, surely He can cover your car payment. Even now He's making provision for you, girl! Trust Him and see.

Lord, thank You for covering my needs—morning, noon, and night! I'm on Your mind, and You're ready to surprise me with supernatural provision! Amen.

UNSTOPPABLE ACCESS TO THE FATHER

*In [Christ Jesus] we have boldness and access
with confidence through our faith in him.*

EPHESIANS 3:12 ESV

Imagine you received an invitation to dine with the Queen of England. You would wear your best dress, pay close attention to your makeup and hair, and be on your very best behavior. No doubt your knees would knock as you approached the dining hall.

Now imagine that her bodyguards turned you away at the last minute, just as you approached. No way! After all of that? Why? Weren't you pretty enough? Good enough? Important enough? Didn't she care about all your prep work? Ugh!

Aren't you glad God isn't like that? He won't turn you away even if you come to Him grimy and naked. He has unstoppable access in mind for you, His daughter. The only thing you have to prep is your heart!

So approach God boldly. Come to Him with confidence. There are no bodyguards to push you aside. There is no CLOSED sign on God's door. He's always open, always available, and always happy to meet with you, His child.

*Thank You for granting me open access, Lord! I've been given such
a gift—time with You! I'm grateful You take me as I am. Amen.*

SEATED AT THE RIGHT HAND OF GOD

*If then you have been raised with Christ, seek the things that
are above, where Christ is, seated at the right hand of God.*

COLOSSIANS 3:1 ESV

At this very moment, Christ is seated at the right hand of God. And
here you are, down on earth, wondering how you're going to make
it through that next crisis. Heaven seems so far away. God feels like
He's a million miles from you. How can you get from here to there?
Would you be welcomed, even if you could reach God's throne?

What remarkable news, to realize that through God's Son, Jesus,
you have instant access to that throne room. You can waltz in there,
lay your needs at the feet of your unstoppable God, and watch as He
performs the miraculous in your heart.

Thanks to the sacrifice of your Savior, unstoppable access is yours,
girl. What a blessing. What a privilege. What an amazing God we serve.

*Thank You for Your work on the cross, Jesus! If not for You, I would
have no access at all. But You provided the key that allows me to
walk into heaven with my requests. I am eternally grateful. Amen.*

NO OTHER DOOR

*Jesus said to [Thomas], "I am the way, and the truth,
and the life. No one comes to the Father except through me."*

JOHN 14:6 ESV

Imagine you're standing in a room with three doors in front of you.
All those doors are closed. You know that one of them will grant you
access to heaven, but you aren't sure which one. You try the first, but
it is locked. You try the second. It is sealed as well. Clearly the third
door is the only way through. So which door will you take?

The answer might seem obvious, but here is a hard fact: Jesus
is the only way to get to heaven. He's the only door that opens and
grants access to humankind. And yet even after hearing this news,
many will choose other doors. They will be closed out of eternity for
simply choosing the wrong way. In these uncertain times, it is more
important than ever to point to Jesus so that everyone knows which
door to take.

*Jesus, You are the Way, the Truth, and the Life. I know
there's no way to heaven except through You. I'm so
grateful for Your work on the cross. Amen.*

THE BLOOD OF JESUS

*Therefore, brothers and sisters. . .we have confidence to enter
the Most Holy Place by the blood of Jesus, by a new and living
way opened for us through the curtain, that is, his body.*

HEBREWS 10:19–20 NIV

Consider this truth: it's the blood of our Savior that grants access into heaven. There is no way around it. Your good works won't get you there. Church attendance won't do it. Being kind to your neighbor? That's a great idea, but it's not going to open the doors of heaven. You have to come through the sacrifice of Jesus on the cross. It's the only way in.

Some might read that and wonder why God chose a bloody route into the kingdom. Couldn't He have come up with a less messy, less painful way? Here's a truth that dates back to the beginning of humankind: good things always require sacrifice.

In this case, Jesus paid the ultimate sacrifice. He shed His blood on the cross so that you could have eternal life. What a gift He gave. And because of this gift, You have 24-7 access beyond the veil!

*Nothing but the blood of Jesus! I know there's no
other way, Lord. Thank You for sending Your Son.
I accept that gift with praise on my lips. Amen.*

BEHIND THE CURTAIN

We have this as a sure and steadfast anchor of the soul,
a hope that enters into the inner place behind the curtain.

HEBREWS 6:19 ESV

Old Testament priests were the only ones who were allowed to enter the Holy of Holies, the place where God dwelled. Ordinary men and women could not. They depended on the priest to (literally) risk his life to visit with God on their behalf. (Hey, back in those days a priest could be struck dead upon entering the Holy of Holies! He never knew if he would come out alive!)

Aren't you glad those days are past? You have access beyond the veil. When Jesus died on the cross, the veil in the temple was torn in two. It was split down the middle. For the first time in forever, ordinary human beings could reach out and touch God. Best of all, you never have to fear retribution. You'll live through it, girl. In fact, you'll come out of it healthier and stronger than before!

This is the gift of the Savior. This is the gift God freely offers to humankind: access beyond the veil. Entering the Holy of Holies. Spending one-on-one time with the Creator of all. What a gift!

Lord, I'm so grateful that the veil was torn in two. I can
walk freely into a place that ordinary people once could not
go. You meet me in the Holy of Holies, arms outstretched.
What an awesome, welcoming God You are. Amen.

ON OUR BEHALF

Christ has entered, not into holy places made with hands,
which are copies of the true things, but into heaven itself,
now to appear in the presence of God on our behalf.

HEBREWS 9:24 ESV

If you've ever been in a courtroom, you know the benefit of having a really good lawyer. It helps so much to have a compassionate and skilled advocate, someone who isn't afraid to approach the judge on your behalf. Truly, a good attorney can mean the difference between life and death for the accused.

This is exactly what we have in the person of Jesus Christ. We have unstoppable access to the King of kings, the Creator of all. Jesus is the best attorney around. Best of all, the fee has already been paid!

You don't have to go through this alone. Whatever you're facing right now, whatever you're most afraid of—let your Advocate take it from here. Take advantage of the access that is yours through the blood of the Savior.

Thank You, my Advocate! What I could not do on my own, You are more than happy to do for me. You approach my heavenly Father on my behalf. What an honor. What a gift. I'm forever grateful. Amen.

ACCESS TO THE FATHER

Through [Christ Jesus] we both have access in one Spirit to the Father.
EPHESIANS 2:18 ESV

Imagine you were placed in a jail cell. As that huge metal door slammed shut, the sound would reverberate across the facility, a message to all that you weren't going anywhere. Only the jailer could release you. He alone held the key.

The enemy of your soul would love nothing more than to keep you bound up, much like a prisoner in a cell. But Jesus holds the key to your release! Through His work on the cross, He gives you complete access to God the Father, to eternal life, and to a blissful stay in heaven when the time comes.

But that's not all! Your unstoppable God has also given you access to all you will need to get through this current life too! He has given you joy for sorrow, peace for pain, and trust for despair. This access that He has granted is truly a key that unlocks every door that ever gets slammed in your face.

Be set free, woman of God! You now have access to all that God has for you.

Thank You, Lord, for setting me free! You hold the keys to life, and I'm so grateful You used them to release me from the things that once bound me!

CONFIDENCE LEADS TO MERCY AND GRACE

Let us then with confidence draw near to the throne of grace,
that we may receive mercy and find grace to help in time of need.

HEBREWS 4:16 ESV

Perhaps you've been through seasons when you were scared to approach God. Maybe you slipped up and fell away for a spell, but now you're back. You want to run into His arms, but you're scared. After all, you broke a few promises to Him. Will He still welcome you back?

You work your way past the fear and propel yourself into His arms. There, in less than a second, He offers all the mercy and grace you ever dreamed of. And in that instant, you realize the truth: your confidence to return to Him led you to a favorable outcome. All He ever wanted was to pour Himself out on your behalf.

What's holding you back from the Savior today? Has it been a while? Have you been in a rebellious season? Have you allowed your hardened heart to keep you away? Today, work up the courage to approach Him no matter what you've done. He will welcome you back with open arms, a heart softened by love.

Thank You for Your unstoppable grace, Lord!
Thank You for Your unstoppable mercy. You've
transformed my heart, and I'm so grateful. Amen.

UNSTOPPABLE PRAYER

The LORD is near to all who call on him, to all who call on him in truth.

PSALM 145:18 ESV

Imagine you had access to a Supreme Court justice. You could call him whenever you liked, even past the midnight hour. You had his personal cell phone number and an open invitation to let him know your needs anytime day or night. No limitation. But instead of contacting him during your moment of crisis, you picked up the phone and called a friend instead. Or maybe you turned to food. Or alcohol. You avoided the one person who could fix the problem for you.

That might sound like an extreme example, but that's exactly what you do when you leave God out of the equation. He's right there, arms extended, granting complete and total access. He has the answers you need. Instead of looking to yourself or to others, turn to Him today.

> *How many times I have forgotten to go to You*
> *first, Lord? I could have avoided so much pain*
> *if only I had taken advantage of the access You*
> *so willingly provided. Thank You for extending*
> *an open invitation. Today, I come! Amen.*

DRAW NEAR

Let us draw near to God with a sincere heart and with the full
assurance that faith brings, having our hearts sprinkled to cleanse us
from a guilty conscience and having our bodies washed with pure water.

HEBREWS 10:22 NIV

Have you ever adopted a puppy that was shy or skittish? Maybe it ran from you instead of leaping into your arms. It can take some time to win over the frightened ones, for sure. They need more TLC, more convincing, more cuddles and tummy tickles.

Your heavenly Father doesn't want you to be shy about approaching Him. He longs for you to draw near, heart filled with faith. (Like a bold puppy!) He's just as gentle as the kindest master, ready to comfort you when you're scared.

It's easy to draw near when you have the assurance of His forgiveness for any sins you've committed. Think of a naughty puppy hiding from its owner. It's scared to draw near because of shame. You, though? There's no reason for shame, for you're a forgiven child of God! He has sprinkled you clean from that guilty conscience. He has washed you white as snow. So approach Him boldly, girl!

Thank You, Lord! My shame days are behind me now. I'll come
boldly to Your throne, confident in Your forgiveness. Amen.

UNSTOPPABLE PRAYER

*"Call to me and I will answer you, and will tell you
great and hidden things that you have not known."*

JEREMIAH 33:3 ESV

God is unstoppable in His passion for you. And because He adores
you, He longs to spend quality time with You. He loves it when you
come to Him in prayer, pouring out your heart and sharing your
daily struggles and joys. In the same way that parents gather with
their children around the dinner table and talk about their day, your
unstoppable God longs to hear it all—the good, the bad, and the ugly.

Don't you love today's verse? God asks you to call to Him. And
He gives you a promise: if you call, He will answer. (Hey, even your
best friend doesn't always pick up the phone!) Best of all, He's not
just interested in hearing what you're going through. He actually has a
response to make things better. He longs to whisper great and hidden
things to your heart. Wow!

Today, spend quality time in prayer with your heavenly Father.

*Lord, thank You for loving me so much! Experiencing Your love makes
me want to spend even more time with You, my unstoppable God! Amen.*

THE SPIRIT INTERCEDES

*In the same way, the Spirit helps us in our weakness. We do
not know what we ought to pray for, but the Spirit himself
intercedes for us through wordless groans. And he who searches
our hearts knows the mind of the Spirit, because the Spirit
intercedes for God's people in accordance with the will of God.*

ROMANS 8:26–27 NIV

Have you ever been in a position that was so precarious, so fragile, that you didn't even know how to pray? Maybe you were so overwhelmed that words just wouldn't come. Or perhaps you felt that you had already prayed at length but still hadn't seen the answers you desired.

Instead of giving up in moments like those, lean in closer to your unstoppable heavenly Father. When you don't know how to pray, His Spirit does. Today's Bible reading has a promise that the Spirit of God will intercede for you. Wow! Have you ever given thought to the notion that God Himself is unstoppable in prayer? He moves through you with words so deep you can't fully express them. (Talk about a holy intervention!)

So when you don't know how to pray or what to pray, open yourself up to the Spirit's intercession with groanings too deep for words.

> *Spirit of God, have Your way in my heart. When I
> don't know what to pray, pray through me. Amen.*

PRAYERS FOR ALL

First of all, then, I urge that supplications, prayers,
intercessions, and thanksgivings be made for all people.

1 TIMOTHY 2:1 ESV

Who do you pray for? Do you keep a prayer list? Your unstoppable God wants you to know that you should be praying not just for those in your inner circle but for people across this globe. Your friends, family, state, country, and all the continents across planet Earth all need prayer. And though you won't have time to break it all down and name every single name every single time, you can lift them up as they come to mind.

Crisis in the Middle East? Pray.

Hurricane along the Gulf Coast? Pray.

Chaos in Washington, DC? Pray.

It doesn't matter who and it doesn't matter where, the answer is always the same. Pray. And don't worry about getting the words right. Some people hyperfocus on how their prayer will be received by God. Girl, He's just so happy to hear from you; He's not fretting over the way the sentences are coming out! (Do you fret over those things when you're hanging out with a close friend? Of course not!)

Just be yourself. Talk to Him. Listen. Then talk to Him some more.

I will be unstoppable in praying, Lord—for those who are close to me
and even for those I don't know personally. When there's a crisis, or
when all is well, I will come to You, my precious heavenly Father. Amen.

JESUS IS PRAYING FOR YOU

Who is to condemn? Christ Jesus is the one who died—
more than that, who was raised—who is at the right
hand of God, who indeed is interceding for us.

ROMANS 8:34 ESV

Isn't it fascinating to think that Jesus Christ, the same One who died for your sins and gave you an opportunity to experience eternity with Him, is in heaven right now, seated at the right hand of the Father, lifting your name in prayer?

Wow! He intercedes for God's children. He's the middleman, taking your needs to the Father. He's the courier, the go-between, the One who knows and cares about everything you are struggling with. And He's more than happy to bear that burden all the way to the Father's listening ear, where He will share with great intensity on your behalf.

If you've ever interceded on behalf of someone else, you know the passion it takes to share their story. How remarkable to think that Jesus speaks with that same passion about you. He truly loves you, girl!

Wow, Jesus! Thank You for interceding on my behalf. I sense Your
love, Your caring. Thank You for intervening for me. Amen.

CONSTANTLY MENTIONING

We give thanks to God always for all of you,
constantly mentioning you in our prayers.

1 THESSALONIANS 1:2 ESV

Some people make it onto our prayer list for short periods of time. Others? They stay on the list for years and years. Their issues are many. Their stumbles and tumbles are numerous.

Maybe you have a few on your list that feel like hard cases. You wonder if you will be taking their names to the Lord every day for the rest of your life. You also secretly wonder if your prayers for them are doing any good.

And then you see a verse like the one in today's devotion. The disciples prayed continually for certain groups of people. Why do you suppose that is? Because people are worthy of that kind of time and attention. Someone needs to stand in the gap for the hard cases, girl. Will that someone be you?

I will be unstoppable in the way I pray for others, Lord.
Never let me forget all the many people who have prayed
for me over the years. Make me an intercessor as well. Amen.

BELIEVE YOU HAVE RECEIVED IT

*"Therefore I tell you, whatever you ask in prayer,
believe that you have received it, and it will be yours."*

MARK 11:24 ESV

Today's verse is rather remarkable. You are admonished to believe even before you receive from God. Does that sound impossible?

Remember the faith you had as a kid? Christmas was approaching and you felt absolutely sure there would be a bicycle under the tree. You had no doubt in your mind, in fact. You could imagine what it would look like, even what it would feel like to climb aboard that bike for the first time and take off down the road. You had faith to believe for every part of that miracle.

God wants you to have that same level of faith when it comes to your prayer requests. He doesn't want you to waver or doubt. The anticipation you experienced as a kid? He wants you to look forward to your miracle the same way.

Be unstoppable in your faith. Even in the face of the naysayers, don't give up. It could be you're on the brink of a miracle even now.

*I won't give up, Jesus! I'll go on believing even before I receive
anything at all from You. I will ask in faith, my heart settled. Amen.*

ABIDE

"If you abide in me, and my words abide in you,
ask whatever you wish, and it will be done for you."

JOHN 15:7 ESV

Have you ever contemplated the word *abide*? When you abide in someone, you're content just to be with them. No doubt you felt like this as a teen when you finally got to spend time with that boy you had a crush on. You didn't have to have any special plans. Just sitting side by side on the sofa having a chat was enough. In fact, you didn't even need to speak. His mere presence was enough to bring joy to your heart.

That's how God feels about hanging out with you! He's unstoppable in His desire to have quality time with you. He's not waiting for you to say something brilliant or to perform for Him. He doesn't need chatter or promises of all the things you plan to do for Him. He simply wants to "be" with you, to abide with you.

So hang out with Him today, girl! Let His words from the Bible settle deep into your heart. Listen closely as He whispers these priceless words: *"Just being with you is enough."*

I will abide in You, my unstoppable God. Your words are hidden
deep in my heart, very much a part of me. I come to You with
confidence, knowing that You desire to be with me. Amen.

PRAY WITHOUT CEASING

Pray without ceasing.

1 THESSALONIANS 5:17 ESV

Perhaps you read today's verse and you wonder, *How, Lord? Am I supposed to stay up twenty-four hours a day, seven days a week, 365 days a year? How in the world am I supposed to pray without ceasing? It makes no sense!*

Look at it this way. Perhaps you have a certain time of day that you enjoy a prayer time. That's great! But to pray without ceasing means that you stop immediately and pray when a situation comes up. You don't say, "I'll add this to my list and get to it tomorrow." No, you start right away, in the moment.

Examples: You pass a bad accident on the road. You call 911 and then start praying. Or you see a social media post that a friend's child is in critical condition. You immediately take that matter to prayer. To pray without ceasing simply means that you're on it. Whenever the need arises, you dive right in. So brace yourself, girl. You'll have a thousand opportunities to pray!

Lord, please quicken my spirit so that I will always be drawn to prayer no matter when, no matter where, no matter who. I'll be ready to pray in the moment! Amen.

SHUT THE DOOR

*"When you pray, go into your room and shut the door
and pray to your Father who is in secret. And your
Father who sees in secret will reward you."*

MATTHEW 6:6 ESV

Have you ever wondered why God gives His kids this biblical instruction to go into their room, shut the door, and pray? Is He saying you shouldn't pray in the kitchen with your family? Is He saying you shouldn't join a prayer circle at church and pray with your friends?

Of course not. Your unstoppable God is simply drawing attention to the fact that some matters are so personal and so intense that they require drawing away from the crowd for a few moments to spend time with Him. When you're alone in your room, you're not distracted. When you shut off your phone or close your tablet, you are free to focus on what really matters.

So draw close to God in the secret place. Then pour your heart out, girl! He's right there, ready to listen and respond.

*I get it, Lord. You want me to separate myself from the
distractions of this life. Today I choose to do just that. Amen.*

DON'T LOSE HEART

[Jesus] told them a parable to the effect that
they ought always to pray and not lose heart.

LUKE 18:1 ESV

"I'm at the point of giving up."

Maybe you've spoken those words. It's easy to reach that point, especially if you've been praying at length for something but it hasn't yet come to pass. Some days you feel like giving up multiple times over—at home, at work, and with the kids. (Ever had one of those days?)

Today's verse shows us our unstoppable Father's heart. Always pray. Don't lose courage. He cares deeply about what's going on deep within us. He knows that the temptation to quit is very real, but He hopes you won't. He's whispering, *"Hang in there, girl!"* in your ear, even now.

Don't lose heart when it looks like everything is against you. Don't lose heart when you're not feeling the best. Don't lose heart when you're exhausted.

Don't lose heart. That's His wish for you, His child.

> *Lord, I'll do my best to hang on even when I don't*
> *feel like it. I won't let the enemy of my soul rob me*
> *of my peace or my joy. I won't lose heart! Amen.*

UNSTOPPABLE PERSEVERANCE

*Blessed is the man who remains steadfast under trial, for
when he has stood the test he will receive the crown of life,
which God has promised to those who love him.*

JAMES 1:12 ESV

Jesus taught us how to be steadfast under trial. He persevered. Our unstoppable Savior carried that cross up Golgotha's hill, stumbling under the weight of it. But He refused to give up.

He persevered in the hours that He hung on the cross for you and me. And He persevered in death, seeing His journey all the way through to the resurrection. At any point, He could have stopped. (Would you blame Him?) He could have said, "This isn't what I signed up for!"

But He didn't. He kept going against all odds. And that's exactly what He's hoping you'll do too. Sure, you're tired. And yes, things are hard. But you can persevere, girl. You can keep going even when you don't feel like it. Learn from His example. Be steadfast. Keep on keeping on.

*I won't give up, Lord! I'll keep going. I'll be steadfast,
perseverance leading the way! I've learned from the best and
will strive to be more like Him with everything I do. Amen.*

PERSEVERE IN LIFE AND DOCTRINE

Watch your life and doctrine closely. Persevere in them,
because if you do, you will save both yourself and your hearers.

1 TIMOTHY 4:16 NIV

You persevere through trials. You persevere past physical and emotional pain. You persevere through ups and downs on the job. But have you ever considered the notion that God also wants you to persevere in life and doctrine?

Take a close look at today's verse. What do you suppose the Lord means when He asks you to watch your life and doctrine closely?

Could it be that in these last days there will be those who try to change God's Word to mean whatever they want it to mean? If you're not deeply rooted in the Word, you might be led astray! But if you're keeping a watchful eye on what you believe, making sure it lines up with the Bible, you won't be easily swept away by the winds of change.

Have sound doctrine. Don't let anyone steal it, girl. You're going to need it more than ever in the coming days.

Lord, I'll persevere in my life and in what I believe. I'm rooted in
You, and no one will pull me away with flighty teachings! Amen.

LAY ASIDE EVERY WEIGHT

Since we are surrounded by so great a cloud of witnesses, let us also lay aside every weight, and sin which clings so closely, and let us run with endurance the race that is set before us.

HEBREWS 12:1 ESV

You never see a runner deliberately picking up weights to carry with him as he runs his race. On the contrary! He dresses in clothing meant to increase his speed and wears only what is absolutely necessary.

We're all running a race, aren't we? Yet many times we reach out to grab unnecessary weights that slow us down. Anger. Fear. Bitterness. Unforgiveness. These are all weights that can trip us up if we're not careful.

God wants you to lay down the weights today so that you can run unfettered. Lay aside those hard feelings. Give up that anger at your coworker. Brush aside those feelings of shame over that thing you wish you hadn't done. Once free, start running! You'll make it through the race with endurance if you shed the extra weight, girl!

Lord, I won't pick up unnecessary weights! Instead, I'll run like a gazelle, filled with endurance for the race set before me. Help me, I pray. Amen.

KEEP ON RUNNING

You need to persevere so that when you have done the
will of God, you will receive what he has promised.

HEBREWS 10:36 NIV

You've seen the videos. A runner loses steam just as he approaches the finish line. He almost doesn't make it over but somehow perseveres and manages to cross that line before collapsing. The crowd cheers, not because he won the grand prize but because of his tenacity.

Watching someone push through the pain to accomplish their goal? Priceless. But not everyone has the endurance to keep going. They give up before nabbing the prize.

No doubt you have felt like that runner many times in your life. You've run out of steam. You know there's a prize at the end of this race you're running, but you wonder if you will make it. Keep going, girl. Don't give up. Persevere. God has a marvelous prize in mind for you on the other side of the finish line. Heaven awaits! Until then, keep on running.

I've been so tempted to give up, Lord! I'm weary. I'm losing steam.
But I won't quit. Just as You were unstoppable in Your pursuit
of me, I will be unstoppable as I run this race for You. Amen.

DOING GOOD

As for you, brothers and sisters, never tire of doing what is good.
2 THESSALONIANS 3:13 NIV

It's one thing to grow weary because you are overtaxing yourself. No doubt you know what that's like: Long hours at work. Lots of stuff going on with the kids at home. Struggles between friends. On and on the list goes.

You try to keep up with it all, often tumbling into bed well past midnight and getting up before the sun rises. But your body is paying a price. The exhaustion is severe. The migraines are growing worse. The joint pain is problematic.

That sort of exhaustion is tough but controllable. It's another thing all together to grow weary doing good things. Maybe you've been praying for that loved one for years but you're ready to give up. Or perhaps you're tired of being the only one in your family who is living right. So you're ready to throw in the towel.

Don't do it, girl! Hang in there. Persevere till the end. It will be worth it when all is said and done.

I do get weary, Lord. I'm not unstoppable in the same way that You are. I can't go twenty-four hours a day, seven days a week. You never meant for me to. Show me how to keep all things in balance. And while You're at it, Lord, please help me not to give up when it comes to doing good. No matter how tired I get. Amen.

WITH ALL PRAYER AND SUPPLICATION

Praying at all times in the Spirit, with all prayer and supplication. To that end, keep alert with all perseverance, making supplication for all the saints.

EPHESIANS 6:18 ESV

Have you ever had a passionate conversation with someone? Maybe you got upset with your child's teacher and decided it was time for a "come to Jesus" meeting. You let her have it, one inflammatory accusation after another, only to find out in the end that the problem was not with the teacher but with your child. Oops. These things happen, but how embarrassing!

That same kind of passion and supplication that you would use in a conversation like that is what God is looking for when you come to Him in prayer. He wants you to pour your heart out. Get that angst out. Lay your burdens at the cross. Don't keep anything inside. He's big enough to handle it. No, really. Think of all the things He's heard from His kids throughout the years.

Persevere through your prayer time as you pour out your heart to Him. Be passionate, girl.

May I be unstoppable, even in my prayer time, Jesus. I want to come to You boldly, passionately, with no fear or trembling. I know I can trust You with my request, Lord! Amen.

HE STARTED IT. HE WILL FINISH IT.

I am sure of this, that he who began a good work in you
will bring it to completion at the day of Jesus Christ.

PHILIPPIANS 1:6 ESV

God always finishes what He starts. Don't believe it? Think of the many times He has come through for you. All those promises that He made when you were a teen? He fulfilled every one. All those times that you felt things wouldn't work out in your twenties. They always somehow miraculously did. Even now He's seeing your current situation to its logical conclusion. (Hey, if He could get those Israelites to the Promised Land, surely He can get you where you need to go!)

Your unstoppable God is a finisher. He doesn't just start off well and leave things hanging. He carries through to the perfect conclusion. And He longs for you to be a finisher too. Don't just start the race with a bang. Be a girl who finishes well, one who will smile at the end of the race and say, "Hey, I stuck with it! Good for me!"

I want to finish well, Jesus. So many times I get off to a
good start but fizzle out before reaching my goal. Help me go
further and further with each new challenge, I pray. Amen.

PERSEVERANCE IS GROWING YOU

Endurance produces character, and character produces hope.

ROMANS 5:4 ESV

Think of a tiny seedling placed in the ground. It is barely hanging on, hardly getting the nutrients it needs. The farmer waters it, adds fertilizer, and tends to it daily, but nothing seems to be happening, at least not right away. Then one day, miraculously, it just takes off and begins to grow. Before long, it's fully in bloom, its vibrant colors drawing the attention of all who pass by. Time did the trick!

The same is true with you when you persevere. Time does the trick! You'll blossom and grow if you don't give up. And so many spiritual nutrients will be yours for the taking as you wait. Perseverance does its perfect work in you, after all. When you endure, it develops godly character inside you, and with godly character comes a precious commodity—hope.

So, keep on keeping on, girl. Hang in there. Don't let anyone or anything stop you. You're about to grow into a mighty woman of God. Soon you'll be in full bloom!

I can feel the changes taking place inside my heart, Lord.
You've been unstoppable in Your quest to grow me into
someone who is more like You. And perseverance is playing
a role! Thank You for the blossoming I see. Amen.

YOU HAVE KEPT HIS WORD

"Because you have kept my word about patient endurance,
I will keep you from the hour of trial that is coming on
the whole world, to try those who dwell on the earth."
REVELATION 3:10 ESV

This world can be a frightening place at times. Wars. Rumors of wars. Pestilence, bickering, racial division. Sometimes it's overwhelming.

No doubt you have a hard time navigating it and persevering through all the craziness. Sometimes it just feels impossible. It's like you're trying to run in quicksand. But when you patiently endure all the pains of this life, when you keep God's Word and stand as a witness to those who are watching, your unstoppable God will guard you and keep you safe. He will cocoon you with His presence. He will reassure you with His love. All because you held on and didn't let go.

It's not easy to hold on right now, Lord. Sometimes I get on social media
and just want to weep when I see the division. But I will hang in
there. There's coming a day when every knee will bow and every tongue
confess. Until then, may I be the voice of reason and love. Amen.

FIRM IN THE FAITH

Be watchful, stand firm in the faith, act like men, be strong.
1 CORINTHIANS 16:13 ESV

Have you ever watched those stalwart guards outside Kensington Palace? They don't crack a smile. They don't wink. They don't nod. They stand at full attention, unmoved by passersby. Nothing can cause them to crack or crumble.

God wants you to be just that firm in your faith. When people pass by and try to trip you up, you're unfazed. When the enemy sticks out his foot to trip you, you stand strong. They might want to see you crack. They might want to see you fail. But God is doing a supernatural, unstoppable work inside you that will keep you standing at attention for the rest of your days.

Be watchful. Stand firm in your faith. You can do this, mighty woman of God! Your heavenly Father has given you everything you need to succeed and more. Just lean in to Him and trust Him for the rest of the journey.

Lord, how I praise You for Your tender, loving care! You've poured out so much. You've given so freely. You've strengthened me from the inside out, my unstoppable God. You've created me in Your image, giving me all I could ever need not just to survive, but to thrive! How grateful I am. Amen.